Ambushed on the Jaguar Trail

Ambushed

on the Jaguar Trail

Hidden Cameras
on the Mexican Border

Jack L. and Anna Mary Childs

RIO NUEVO PUBLISHERS
TUCSON, ARIZONA

To our children, grandchildren, and great-grandchildren,
who keep us young and share with us the wonders of the trail.

I want to hear Mexican wolves howl once again in the Altar Valley,
but I also want those ranchers to keep on running their cattle on public lands.
Biological diversity may be the new mantra, but cultural heritage needs to be
preserved as well. We should be seeking balances, not exclusion.

—Thomas E. Sheridan, *Arizona: A History*, 1995

7/18/06   4:59 AM   BJDP 56

Contents

Prologue

To "ambush" is to lie in wait in order to launch a surprise attack, to ensnare, or to waylay. The word evokes scenes from an old Western movie. The background music tells us when the hero will be ambushed by the bad guy. However, as we think of an ambush along the jaguar trail, we are no longer dealing with good guys and bad guys. We are now referring to an entirely different kind of ambush. We first use "ambush" to refer to our being ambushed by the jaguar.

In the summer of 1996, Jack was a retired land surveyor. Anna taught school and was preparing for another year at Grijalva Elementary School in Tucson.

We owned three mules and a pack of lion dogs. Jack used his dogs when he hunted mountain lions. We had five Southwest-bred lion hounds with us that day—a breed well suited for hunting large predators in the rugged mountains of the arid southwestern United States.

OPPOSITE: The natural "funnel" formed by the cliffs in this photo makes a good place for an ambush.

Though Anna no longer went on the hunts, she still loved to trail ride with friends and grandchildren in nearby Tucson Mountain Park. Occasionally, she persuaded Jack to go riding with her in more remote areas. We decided to take a leisurely trail ride that August morning, but our morning jaunt became a turning point in our lives. This was the morning we were "ambushed" by "El Tigre," the jaguar. This elusive, mystical animal surprised and delighted us when we met him in August 1996 and continues to lead us down a path filled with adventure, rewards, and disappointment. This path eventually led us to a nearly full-time job in jaguar research and conservation.

El Tigre definitely ambushed us. We now set our hidden cameras along secret pathways with the hope that El Tigre will reveal himself again. Our camera traps are designed to capture the jaguar's image as gently and unobtrusively as possible. We vow to protect his privacy by not revealing any locations to the public, for both their safety and that of the jaguar. Our goal is to learn about his personal life, preferred habitat, and diet, as well as to gain insights into his behavior. El Tigre himself is responsible for the formation of the Borderlands Jaguar Detection Project. He is also responsible for the data generated by this research. He is responsible for giving us insight into the lives of the other animals that he interacts with and depends upon for survival.

Twelve years have passed since we were ambushed by the jaguar. From one event in time, we grew and learned and changed. Since that eventful day in 1996, our horizons have expanded. From our thousands of photos emerge stories, experience, and information. Our desire is to use our knowledge, experiences, and discoveries to educate and enlighten our readers. No one knows what new insights we will gain as we continue to ambush—and be ambushed by—borderland wildlife.

CHAPTER 1

Jaguar Morning

When my eyes finally focused
on him, I saw that he was a
magnificent animal.

JACK: At 7:00 a.m. on August 31, 1996, something happened to us that
changed our lives.

ANNA: It began like an ordinary August morning in southern Arizona. Jack
and I drove out of Tucson in our truck, pulling a gooseneck horse trailer
loaded with mules and hounds. In the pre-dawn darkness, we munched on
fried-egg sandwiches and sipped hot coffee as we headed south.

The sky turned a brilliant pink as we drove to the end of the road and
parked our truck. Our friends Matt and Gavin pulled up behind us. These
two young men were almost as eager as the hounds to begin exploring the
trail that wound ahead. The cool, humid air clung to us as we climbed out of
our trucks. It was time to saddle mules and begin our pre-sunrise ride into
the rugged nearby mountains.

JACK: At 5:00 a.m. Matthew Colvin, my wife, Anna Mary, and I saddled up the mules and turned our hounds loose to make an early morning ride in the Baboquivari Mountains southwest of Tucson. Gavin Weller, a young taxidermist, was also with us as we rode out in the fresh mountain air.

I had been running big game with hounds since 1964, and up until that day I thought I had seen everything. At that time of year our daytime temperatures commonly exceed 100 degrees F. This was to be a short hunt, designed to exercise the hounds and keep their feet from getting soft over the summer.

ANNA: The hounds bayed impatiently. They were ready to explore and enjoy this rare change from the heat of Tucson and the confinement of their pens. We all needed a break from a long, hot Arizona summer. This was to be a recreational, fun ride. Chasing a cat was not on our agenda.

The sky lightened as we saddled the mules. Jack opened the dog boxes. Surrounded by leaping hounds, we rode up the trail on this beautiful summer morning.

JACK: We rode out that morning in the pre-dawn darkness. We hoped to make ten or twelve miles before it became too hot.

ANNA: The August monsoon rains had worked their magic. The normally dry, barren hills and canyons were covered with lush vegetation. The humid air became warmer as the sun rose higher in the sky.

Almost invisible gnats and other flying insects filled the air. Wild blue morning glory and scarlet creeper of brilliant orange wove together into a tangle of color. The canyon was alive with beauty, birdsong, and the sounds of rushing water.

We continued to ride. Our trail gradually wound up out of the canyon and onto the steep, rocky mountain that loomed ahead. The hounds ran ahead of us, noses scouring the ground searching for the scent of a mountain lion. Suddenly their voices rang out. Jack and Matt knew that the dogs had struck a track. "Probably a mountain lion," Jack remarked. Matt agreed that they should let the dogs run the track. I was silently thinking that our "relaxing" ride had just come to an abrupt end.

JACK: After traveling about two miles, the hounds struck a cold track. The ground was hard and dry, making it difficult for the hounds to trail and for us to find a track. As all five of the hounds were trained to trail only lions, we decided to let them work and see what happened. Eventually we found a few partial tracks and decided we were trailing a large male lion and that we were trailing it in the right direction. By this time, the hounds had moved the track about a mile, and all five hounds were working.

We rode up a canyon with a good horseback trail running through the bottom. The upper end of this canyon is extremely rough and steep, with many large rocks, juniper trees, and oak brush. This trail turns out of the canyon and climbs to the ridge top on the left-hand side. It continues up the ridge parallel to the canyon. Anna and I stopped at the place where the trail turns out of the canyon. Matt and Gavin followed the hounds into the rough country.

ANNA: Matt and Gavin galloped ahead of us, following the faint and barely audible sounds of the hounds. We tied up the mules and waited when the trail leading up the mountain became nearly impassable. The sun burned down on us. The mules flicked away the gnats and flies with their tails and patiently waited in the warm, sticky air. We heard the hounds jump something high on the ridge above us. Suddenly their voices changed to a rapid, staccato chop as they announced that they had brought their quarry to bay.

JACK: We could hear the hounds well from our vantage point. After about half an hour, it sounded as if they had found where the cat had made a kill. They would work off in one direction, make a short circle, and end up back in the same pocket. After doing this several times, they trailed into some bluffs and jumped the cat from its daytime resting place. After a short race, they treed. Anna and I started up the canyon bottom on the mules. In just a short distance, traveling became extremely difficult. Anna decided she had gone far enough. She said, "I've seen lions before and I'm going to tie up this mule and sit in the shade until you get back."

ANNA: Jack strapped on his video camera, grabbed a fresh supply of film, and started up the canyon on foot. He soon met Gavin, who was coming down to get us. Gavin told him that the hounds had treed a jaguar.

JACK: I tied up, grabbed my video camera, and continued on foot. I soon passed Matt's and Gavin's mules tied to a tree. A short time later, I met Gavin coming back down the canyon. He said, "Matt sent me back for some more film and to tell you to hurry on up there because those hounds have just treed a jaguar." Well, to say that I was amazed would be an understatement. The late Dale Lee, legendary jaguar hunter of world fame, had told me many stories about the ferocity of the jaguar. I was wondering why it had stayed treed so long. I told Gavin that I was going to hurry on up to the tree with the video camera and asked him if he would go down the canyon and get Anna. I sure didn't want her to miss this. Gavin agreed to do this and I took off for the tree.

ANNA: Gavin hiked down to the spot where I waited with the mules, as Jack continued on up the mountain. "Go ahead," I told him. "I'll be right behind you." With no trail to follow, I traveled in the direction of the dogs' voices. I pulled and dragged myself up the steep, boulder-strewn mountainside. I forgot about gnats, flies, heat, and humidity in my effort to reach the jaguar before he left the tree.

JACK: That was the longest short climb of my life. When I finally arrived, I could see the hounds and Matt. They were all looking up into this juniper tree. I did not see the jaguar at first glance, so well did he blend in with the tree and surrounding hillside.

When my eyes finally focused on him, I saw that he was a magnificent animal. He was lying on a limb, rear end at the trunk, with both hind legs and one front leg hanging down. He rested his head on the limb with his other paw tucked beneath his head. Comparing the size of the cat's head to the size of his body, we concluded that it was a male.

We spent the next thirty or forty minutes videotaping the scene. We praised the dogs and admired one of God's magnificent and secretive creatures. This is the only live wild jaguar ever videotaped in the United States. At one point, still with his head on his paw, the jaguar closed his eyes and took a short nap. It was as if he were saying, "All right boys, this is boring me. If you would finish your pictures and leave, I will be on my way." Suddenly, his ears perked up, and he opened his eyes and looked off in the direction of the canyon. In a few minutes, Anna arrived.

ANNA: I climbed out of the steep ravine onto the hillside. My eyes gradually focused on the three men and the pack of hounds. They all were staring upward into the branches of a large alligator juniper tree.

There on a high branch was a large jaguar. His belly was full. He was stretched out on the branch, calmly gazing down at the leaping hounds. He was camouflaged perfectly against the branches and leaves of the alligator juniper tree. I pinched myself to be sure I wasn't dreaming. I no longer complained inwardly about the end of our pleasure ride. Instead of feeling regretful, I was overcome by a sense of amazement and thanksgiving for the privilege of being a part of the adventure.

JACK: We spent another twenty minutes photographing and admiring the jaguar. Then we decided we had better leave. The temperature was climbing and the hounds were growing hoarse from lack of water. We knew that we had pushed our luck far enough. The last thing we wanted was to have a confrontation with this cat, especially since jaguars are protected by Arizona law. We leashed the hounds, said "Adios" to Mr. Tigre, and went off down the canyon to the mules. We all felt that God had truly blessed us with this chance-of-a-lifetime encounter.

ANNA: Our ordinary morning became our "jaguar morning." Each sight and sound that led up to the moment of discovery of the jaguar is etched in our memories. We had found a treasure that we didn't seek. We forgot all that was daily and routine as we gazed up at this animal with its massive head and paws. Our relaxing morning ride had turned into one of the most thrilling adventures of our lifetime.

All too soon we called the dogs and left the jaguar in the tree. We said our good-byes and wished the jaguar well. We wanted to believe that the jaguar would be safe and free to roam this harsh mountainous region for many years to come.

Incredibly, we were not the only folks lucky enough to see a jaguar in the borderlands that year. Just six months prior to our encounter, professional hunters Warner Glenn and his daughter, Kelly Glenn Kimbro, were hunting mountain lions in the Peloncillo Mountains along the Arizona/New Mexico border. Their hounds brought to bay an adult male jaguar on a rocky cliff. Instead of reaching for his rifle, Warner reached for his camera and took several photographs before he gathered his dogs, tipped his hat, and rode away. This was the first time a jaguar had ever been photographed alive in the wild in the United States. Warner subsequently published these photos in a book called *Eyes of Fire*. Amazingly, in February 2006, the hounds of Warner and Kelly bayed another jaguar in the "bootheel" region of New Mexico.

Authors Jack and Anna Childs.

CHAPTER 2

The "Jag" Team

We really didn't have any idea
of what we were getting into.

The jaguar was virtually unknown in the desert environment of the American Southwest in 1996. Historical records suggested a small and declining population until the 1940s. After this time, only an occasional jaguar was reported, about every ten years. The species was generally thought to be absent from the area and was not protected by the Endangered Species Act. With these two sightings bringing national attention to the jaguar, the Arizona Game and Fish Department recognized the need for new jaguar conservation strategies. Together with the New Mexico Department of Game and Fish, they created the Arizona-New Mexico Jaguar Conservation Team in 1997. This volunteer team of state and federal wildlife and land-management agencies, university biologists, conservation groups, local landowners, ranchers, and concerned citizens was formed to collaborate in protecting and managing the jaguar in Arizona and New Mexico.

Jack attended the first public meetings and soon became actively involved in this innovative concept of wildlife management. Anna was an interested participant after her retirement from teaching in May of 1998. Held two to four times yearly in locations in both Arizona and New Mexico, the meetings focus on the cutting edge of jaguar conservation and are sometimes charged with heated debates. In the true spirit of cooperative conservation, we strive to overcome our differences and have nicknamed ourselves the "jag team."

The first action items of the jag team included writing protocols to promote jaguar conservation: a jaguar-sighting questionnaire, a kill-verification form, and a track-documentation kit. In an open-dialogue forum, jaguar conservation needs were identified and subcommittees formed to address each area. Arizona Game and Fish also established a jaguar page on its website.

Educating students and the public about jaguar conservation was considered a number-one priority. The education committee developed a packet and other materials for elementary students in grades five through eight, using jaguar facts as a baseline and addressing the Endangered Species Act. The packet is now used in selected elementary schools in Arizona, and the material was recently translated into Spanish.

To reach other borderland residents, an educational "outreach committee" conducted educational presentations in communities in southeastern Arizona and southwestern New Mexico. A slide show was followed by an open-forum panel discussion by representatives of the Defenders of Wildlife, the Sky Island Alliance, the ranching community, and various federal and state land-management agencies. Jack was the keynote speaker for these forums, and Anna attended all of these meetings. The community members who attended were enthusiastic and interested in the jaguar. Our audiences ranged in number from twenty to fifty people, from very young children to elderly

Federal Protection for the Jaguar

Soon after the formation of the jag team, an important event took place. On January 31, 1997, the United States Fish and Wildlife Service declared the jaguar an endangered species in Arizona and New Mexico. To encourage jaguar management at the local level, U.S. Fish and Wildlife gave the Arizona and New Mexico game departments the authority to implement jaguar conservation strategies, following recommendations of the jag team.

Next, the Arizona Game and Fish Department successfully advocated for Arizona's Senate Bill 1106 in 1998, imposing a $2,500 criminal penalty (Class 2 misdemeanor) and up to $72,500 in civil penalties for the unlawful killing of a jaguar. A similar bill (Senate Bill 252) was enacted in New Mexico in 1999. These state laws take effect only if the jaguar is removed from the federal endangered species list. In 2006 the New Mexico legislature passed and signed into law House Bill 536 ("Unlawful Trophy Animal Disposition"), allowing the New Mexico Game Commission to authorize higher civil damages than previously allowable for wildlife designated as trophy animals, and establishing a minimum $2,000 in civil penalties (without requiring removal from ESA listing to take effect). Thus, higher penalties for illegal jaguar killing may be established through commission action, although no such action had been taken as of this writing in 2007.

citizens. Their questions were challenging and thought-provoking. At one particularly crowded meeting, the local citizens kept arriving after the program began. It eventually became standing room only, with several people sitting on the floor along the wall. We were definitely over the fire code but no one seemed to worry, and it made for a very energetic evening.

The jag team asked Jack to chair the "research committee." This group of biologists and others who are knowledgeable about jaguars wrote a complete jaguar study design. Using jaguar locations from the historical record, the "habitat committee" produced a map delineating potential suitable jaguar habitat.

Jack also chairs the "depredation committee," whose task is to investigate any loss of livestock attributed to jaguars. If a kill is verified as the work of a jaguar, the owner of the livestock would then be reimbursed for the loss with money from a fund established by the Malpai Borderlands Group—a well-known ranch-community-based group, profiled in Nathan Sayre's book *Working Wilderness*. Their goal is "to restore and maintain the natural processes that create and protect a healthy, unfragmented landscape to support a diverse, flourishing community of human, plant and animal life in our borderlands region." Warner Glenn, one of the founders of the Malpai Borderlands Group and a member of the jag team's depredation committee, donated money from funds generated by the sale of his book *Eyes of Fire*.

Warner, Matt Colvin, and Jack shared the responsibility of conducting field investigations of any reported kills. At this point, we had no real idea what a jaguar kill looked like. We could not distinguish a jaguar track from that of a mountain lion. In reviewing all the available jaguar literature, we found little that pertained to the jaguar diet or methodology that jaguars use to kill and consume their prey at this northern latitude.

Fortunately, the Phoenix Zoo stepped up and offered to send Matt and Jack to the Pantanal in Brazil, where the zoo was funding a jaguar depredation study. The Pantanal, a 200,000-square-kilometer floodplain made up mostly of privately owned cattle ranches in western Brazil, still supports a viable breeding population of jaguars. This trip was made in May of 1998 with funding from the Phoenix Zoo, the Malpai group, and Arizona Game and Fish.

We were extremely fortunate to have opportunities to gather data about jaguars and jaguar depredation while in the Pantanal. We were able to dissect and analyze the carcasses of four Brahma cattle that had been killed by jaguars. We also documented tracks and other sign left by jaguars. As an added bonus, on eight different occasions we observed wild jaguars in the field. Later that year, Jack published the results of this trip in a field guide, *Tracking the Felids of the Borderlands*. This guide is designed to aid the naturalist in interpreting evidence of the presence of large carnivores along the border of the southwestern United States and Mexico. It focuses primarily on the differences in the habits and methods of depredation between the American mountain lion and the jaguar. Arizona Game and Fish made it possible for this guide to be translated into Spanish, and they are now distributing it to biologists and educators throughout Mexico, as well as Central and South America.

You might wonder what Anna was doing while Jack and Matt roamed the wilds of the Pantanal in Brazil. After driving to Sky Harbor Airport in Phoenix and saying good-bye to the two adventurers, she returned to Tucson and packed up her classroom. She was saying good-bye to her second-grade students as well as to teaching.

Telephone service between Tucson and the Pantanal was sketchy, and the three-hour time difference was a factor. Anna heard from Jack after he arrived in Brazil and then decided that no news was good news. She trusted that he hadn't been eaten by a jaguar or bitten by a venomous snake. One day after he was safely home, she received a letter postmarked "Brazil." Even though he beat the letter home, his words on paper made the adventure even more real to those who remained at home.

The depredation committee later drew up guidelines for the handling of jaguars—either injured animals or for the purpose of attaching a radio tracking collar. Upon completion, these recommendations were presented to

the directors of the Arizona and New Mexico Game and Fish Departments and the United States Fish and Wildlife Service. As of this writing, in August 2007, the jag team is awaiting the decision of the agencies.

Early on, the jag team assembled a scientific advisory group, which consisted of the top jaguar biologists in the United States, Mexico, Central America, and South America. This advisory group recommended that the team initiate a study designed to monitor jaguars along the border and to attempt to determine if there was a resident population of jaguars in the United States.

It was apparent that we needed a full-time biologist who could conduct an in-depth search for the elusive jaguar. During the three years following our jaguar encounters, Warner Glenn and Jack monitored a few remote sensor cameras in the vicinity of the two 1996 sightings. Due to limited time and resources, this surveillance effort was somewhat sporadic and haphazard, and we found no jaguars.

No biologist wants to invest several years of time in a project that may not yield any data. The end-of-year report would likely read, "Again no jaguars found this year." What we needed was someone with big-cat experience who was stubborn, persistent, and used to devoting long hours in a pursuit that yielded few rewards. Someone such as a houndsman. Having a low IQ would help. "I blushed with pride," Jack recalled afterward, "as all eyes turned on me."

Anna recalls now that we were both very naïve about embarking on a project aimed at the detection of jaguars along the southern border. Neither of us was a trained biologist. We really didn't have any idea of what we were getting into. She admits to being in it for the perks along the way. Hiking to and from the cameras always presented the possibility of a rare flower or bird sighting—and a few things we would never have imagined.

10/07   6:55 AM   BJDP 64

CHAPTER 3

The Camera Traps

The cameras allow us to observe breeding behavior, diet, population trends, hours of activity, and much more.

In January 2001, the Wildlife Conservation Society gave Jack a small grant to help initiate a more systematic survey for jaguars in southeastern Arizona. We named this study the Borderlands Jaguar Detection Project (BJDP). Working as a team, hiking and looking for sign together, Jack and Anna began the research for the BJDP in March of that year.

We looked for the presence of jaguars by using remote sensor cameras. Jack decided where the cameras would be placed by relying on his knowledge of mountain lion behavior, acquired over more than forty years of experience following them in the remote mountain ranges of southeastern Arizona. We followed predetermined routes along canyon bottoms, dirt roads, and trails (where large cats were likely to travel) while hiking to each camera to change film and batteries. These defined routes are called "transects" by biologists and are used to survey the same area on a regular basis and record sign—such as tracks, scat, and scent marks—left by the species of wildlife they are studying. Our target species was the jaguar, but we also recorded sign left by lions, bears, and bobcats. We would hike or ride our mules every six weeks as we checked each transect and camera. We began by monitoring twelve transects with twelve motion-sensor cameras.

Tracing lion tracks.

Using a handheld Palm Pilot and a program called Cyber Tracker, we recorded GPS (global positioning system) position, species and type of sign, tracking and weather conditions, and other data, and then when we returned home, we downloaded this information to a database in our computer. We did this for a period of five years. (Photo data on all the species, as well as data on tracks, scat, and scrapes for jaguars in particular, continue to be collected today, on an ongoing basis, by a biologist who has since been added to the project.)

Though we hiked the same distances each time, each trip was a different adventure. Hiking in June is quite different from hiking in November, even though the same animals were out there (except that black bears hibernate in winter, and the bird species vary with the seasons). Flowers bloom in abundance in the spring and summer if we are fortunate enough to have good seasonal rains. We would drive to the site before sunup, sipping coffee and munching our fried-egg sandwiches. We always began our hikes with an unspoken anticipation: "What will we see or find today?" And we were never disappointed. As when we discovered the Baboquivari jaguar in 1996, we never expected what we found. We like to consider our discoveries as "gifts" along the way, and each discovery seemed to lead to another.

The focus of the BJDP is twofold. First, is there a population of jaguars in southern Arizona? If so, what are the dynamics of that population: Are they residents or merely dispersing immigrants from a population in Mexico? If they are residents, what is the size of their home range? What do they eat? What types of habitat do they prefer? Most important, do we have a viable breeding population in Arizona?

Geographically, the study is confined to an area within twenty miles of the Arizona–Mexico border, and from the crest of the Baboquivari Mountains east to the Arizona–New Mexico border. We conduct most of

Measuring a jaguar track.

7/25/07 7:57 PM   BJDP-JB3f

ABOVE: This jaguar was photographed with an infrared camera, which doesn't use a flash and is therefore undetectable.

OPPOSITE PAGE (CLOCKWISE FROM TOP LEFT): One camera catches four different species passing by the same spot—humans, a deer, mountain lions, and a jaguar.

our work in the Coronado National Forest and the Buenos Aires National Wildlife Refuge, but with the owners' permission, we also work on three private ranches in the Baboquivari Mountains.

This is big-cat habitat, made up of steep, rugged mountains with deep bluffy canyons and thick brush interspersed with clearings. This checkerboard landscape is called "edge" by wildlife biologists and creates feeding areas that are close to hiding areas and bedding areas for white-tailed deer, the big cat's favorite prey.

The Cameras

Photography is a key element in the study. Employing a technique known to wildlife biologists as "camera traps," we place cameras along game trails and water sources likely to be used by large felids. We try to locate our cameras in the most remote areas in order to maintain a semblance of secrecy and to minimize human-caused vandalism. (In spite of this precaution, our cameras have recorded a lot of unexpected human activity, as you will see in a later chapter.) The cameras are activated by sensing motion and body heat. After the camera is set and aimed, we perform a walk-through test. After six weeks, we return to change the batteries and install fresh film or a new memory card. A description of each photo is then entered into a database for later analysis.

Even though equipped with a flash, the camera does not appear to frighten the subjects. We have numerous night shots of many species, including the jaguar, that show no evidence of fear or surprise on the part of the animal being photographed. We have captured many large felids on film, as well as a vast array of other wildlife. The cameras are non-invasive, allowing us to discover much about the animal's personal life and behavior in the wild without disturbing the animal with our presence. When humans observe wildlife, we are usually limited to watching the animals flee or

display behaviors that are designed to protect their young. The non-intrusive cameras allow us to observe breeding behavior, diet, population trends, hours of activity, and much more. This is especially true in observing behavior among family groups, as you will see in chapters to follow.

———

Jaguars are considered an "umbrella" species (a term biologists use to denote a wide-ranging species whose conservation would automatically conserve many other species) and are the main focus of our study. However, they are only one element in a much bigger and fascinating ecosystem. We have collected over 15,000 photographs of the animals, ranging from jaguars to squirrels, that call these borderlands home. As we studied the interactions of these animals and their environment, we gained knowledge and new insights into the creatures of the Madrean evergreen woodlands and grasslands of southern Arizona. Imagine our anticipation when our developed film arrived in the mail! We never knew what a roll of film held. Whether it was a pesky blue jay, a curious bear, a mountain lion with cubs, or the elusive jaguar, we were always rewarded when we viewed the photos.

Over the next three years, we received additional small grants from the Phoenix Zoo, the Malpai Borderlands Group, and the Wildlife Conservation Society. In 2004, we qualified for a Heritage Grant through Arizona Game and Fish, which enabled us to add a real biologist to our team: Emil McCain, a young graduate student from Humboldt State University, signed on in June 2004. With experience studying jaguars as a field biologist in Costa Rica and Sonora, Mexico, and with youthful enthusiasm and energy, he expanded the project to forty-five cameras.

Emil is now analyzing six years' worth of camera data while writing his master's thesis on the daily activity patterns of large carnivores and their prey.

Emil—with his phenomenal tracking skills and analytical abilities—is a great asset to the project. He is in charge of all the fieldwork and is instrumental in obtaining grants to fund the project. Monies received from the Disney Foundation, Woodland Park Zoo, and Humboldt University's "Save the Jaguar" Fund go toward equipment and a modest stipend for Emil—your typical dedicated, starving biologist trying to make ends meet. The jag team soon recognized his expertise, and he is now also a member of its scientific advisory group.

Verifying Potential Sightings

The job of verifying potential jaguar sightings called in by the public fell to the two state Game and Fish Departments and the BJDP. Game and Fish asked Jack to follow up on many of these calls by talking with the observers. Jack also conducted on-site investigations in which he searched for tracks and any other evidence left by the animal. At times the area would be too rocky and vegetated for the animal to leave a track, or the exact geographical area could not be determined. At other times he was able to find clear tracks, which usually turned out to be those of a mountain lion, bobcat, or sometimes even a domestic dog. Young lions are often misidentified as jaguars due to their long tails and spots.

Even the spotted bobcat has been misidentified because of its "long" tail (most people envision the bobcat as having a two-inch stub of a tail, when in fact the length is from six to eight inches). One caller reported finding a dead "ocelot" (a small felid similar in size to a bobcat, rare in the Southwest, with jaguar-like markings and a thirteen-inch tail) lying beside the trail in the bottom of Aravaipa Canyon. When we asked about the length of the tail, we were informed that it was "long." After a three-mile hike, we found a dead bobcat at the coordinates given by the observer. Interestingly, this bobcat had

A coyote is caught by an infrared camera.

BJDP-JB6

been killed by a female mountain lion. There were canine-tooth puncture marks in the bobcat's head. Tracks of the lion and a cub were found near the bobcat carcass and around the nearby covered carcass of a whitetail buck that the lion had killed. The bobcat was probably attempting to steal a free meal, and this mother lion was simply defending her kill and protecting the life of her cub.

Many reports claim to document observations of black jaguars. The black or melanistic phase of the jaguar occurs more frequently in certain areas of South America, and is rare in Central America. According to researchers David Brown and Carlos López González, "Black or melanistic jaguars have never been documented in the wild north of Mexico's Isthmus of Tehuantepec, with the exception of captive animals which are commonly bred in zoos." Under certain light conditions any animal could be perceived as black. Anna has often overheard Jack answer the phone and then ask a caller, "Was it black?" She knows instantly that the caller saw something—but not a jaguar. Jack will continue to view these sightings with skepticism until a photograph of a black jaguar turns up that is verifiable as being taken in Sonora or the southwestern United States.

In our experience, black Labrador retrievers are the animals most commonly mistaken for black jaguars. We once received a picture on our computer, taken in northern Arizona, purportedly of a black jaguar walking across a mountain meadow. It was later confirmed by Game and Fish, after an on-site investigation, that the black "jaguar" was in reality a very large black house cat. Upon examining the photo it was found that the two- to four-inch-high grass of the meadow came up past the cat's belly. We have also examined several plaster casts of tracks that were assumed to be made by jaguars but were either of a mountain lion or a large dog. (Some of the casts were too poorly made or the track was not clear enough for positive identification.)

The number of sightings always increases after a jaguar is shown on local television or in newspapers. Most "sightings" are within a twenty-five-mile radius of downtown Tucson, some even within the city limits. To date, none of the reported sightings have been verifiable as jaguars. This is not surprising, since jaguars at this latitude are almost strictly nocturnal and seldom venture out in daylight.

Although we investigate these calls with skepticism, we don't want to discourage anyone from calling. We are forever hopeful that the next call will turn out to be the real thing.

Notice the length of the bobcat's tail, the cause of many mistaken "jaguar" sightings.

All in the Family

═══

Clearly, the jaguar is a rare
and colorful symbol of a
much larger web of wildlife.

While we waited for jaguar sightings, we learned about many other animals
that live in this borderlands region. As you will see in the following
chapters, our cameras provided some wonderful insights into their family
life, methods of communication, periods of peak activity, breeding habits,
and predator-prey behavior. We observed the effects of drought and fire on
the environment, and we also collected some fascinating information on
human behavior, underlining the fact that *Homo sapiens* is a part of this
ecosystem too. Clearly, the jaguar is a rare and colorful symbol of a much
larger web of wildlife, for without a fully functioning ecosystem to support
it, no top predator such as the jaguar can possibly survive.

Although the Southwestern borderlands lie a long way north of the
tropics—defined as the geographical zone between the Tropics of Cancer

and Capricorn—this ecosystem contains a number of neotropical species, including the jaguar. Over the past sixty million years, Earth's climate has changed from a warmer, wetter environment to the cooler and drier conditions found today. However, this warmer, wetter climate is still found in the New World south of the Tropic of Cancer; neotropical plants and animals are those species that are more at home in the hot, humid regions yet sometimes extend their range beyond them. Southeastern Arizona, up to the Gila River, is at the northern edge of the home range of many of these neotropical plant and animal communities. Neotropical birds such as the elegant trogon and the sulphur-bellied flycatcher call this area home in the summer months, and neotropical mammals including javelina, coati, Mexican brown-nosed opossum, hog-nosed skunk, and birds such as Gould's turkey are year-round residents. The jaguar, although never abundant, was also once considered a year-round resident. Neotropical species make up a large proportion of our local flora and fauna, and their survival is very important to this unique ecosystem.

Evidence of successful reproduction is a good indicator of a healthy ecosystem. The parent animal requires an adequate supply of prey or plant life to successfully raise offspring. The young animals, in turn, furnish prey for other members of the ecosystem. This may be an over-simplification of the circle of life, but read on for a glimpse into the intimate family lives of coatis, javelinas, opossums, white-tailed deer, bobcats, black bears, and mountain lions.

In the carnivore family, only the wild canids form biparental family bonds. Both the male and female fox, coyote, and wolf share in the feeding of their offspring. For reasons unknown to us, our cameras never captured images of fox or coyote pups. Wolves do not inhabit the study area.

Two neotropical species: javelina and Mexican brown-nosed opossum.

White-nosed coati *(Nasua narica)*

The coati, a raccoon-like animal with a long nose and long erect tail, lives and travels in family groups (called troops) of five to fifty animals consisting of females and their offspring. At times, two troops may temporarily combine around an abundant food source, giving the impression of a much larger group. Female coatis weigh an average of nine pounds, while the average male weighs around twelve pounds. The male lives a solitary life and visits the troop only in his search for females in estrus. Females give birth in late June to litters of three to six kits.

The first coati recorded in Arizona was at Fort Huachuca in 1892. Coati observations became more frequent by the 1920s and 1930s in southeastern Arizona, probably because their numbers increased due to climatic factors and perhaps fire suppression. White-nosed coatis occur from Panama north to southeastern Arizona, southwestern New Mexico, and Texas along the Rio Grande. A related species, the ring-tailed coati, lives in South America.

Coatis are sometimes mistakenly called "coatimundi," from the Tupian Brazilian Indian words *coati* (meaning "belt-nosed") and *mundi* ("loner"). This name was given to the male coati due to its solitary nature (see bottom right photo). It was thought at one time that the male was a separate species, but we now know that they are the opposite gender of the same species.

Mountain lions, bobcats, jaguars, black bears, and the golden eagle prey upon coatis. They avoid these predators by being active only during daylight hours (diurnal) and sleeping in tall trees or rocky cliffs at night.

Omnivores, the coati's diet consists almost entirely of fruits such as juniper berries and invertebrates such as beetles and caterpillars. They dig through leaf litter on the forest floor searching for these items, making the area look as if it had been roto-tilled. Coatis also climb the stalks of the century plant to feed on the pollen and nectar contained in the flower.

ANNA: Close Encounter with a Coati

Every six weeks we hiked to the cameras to change film and batteries, and along the way we recorded evidence of sign (tracks, scat, or scrapes) left by large carnivores. We never knew what we would find or see—and some days were more exciting than others.

One sunny day in June, we walked up a canyon looking for tracks and other animal sign. I was walking along the sandy creek bottom while Jack surveyed the trail that paralleled the creek. We each carried a walking stick made by Jack from a stalk of sotol. Sotol (*Dasylirion wheeleri*), commonly called "desert spoon," is a member of the lily family. Similar in appearance to yucca, it blooms in the Arizona desert from May through August. The blossoms are small and grow on a tall stalk that rises above the cluster of leaves growing close to the ground. When the flowers finish blooming, the stalk dies and falls to the ground.

Suddenly we heard a piercing, eerie cry. I first thought it might be some kind of hawk, but then I saw a coati several yards to my left. Not only was he the source of the piercing cry, but he was moving in a very peculiar way. Every few minutes he would sit on his haunches and rock back and forth as if in some kind of agony. He moved down the hill on my left and across our path in the direction of some large metal water storage tanks. At this point, I retreated up the trail where I watched from a "safe" distance. Jack followed the animal, video camera in hand. The coati walked to the tank and began scratching as if searching for water.

By now we suspected that this animal could be rabid. I shouted, telling Jack to come away from harm's way, but he continued to film. The coati then turned and made a beeline for Jack, continuing to utter its shrill cry. As Jack ran back down the trail, he glanced back and discovered that the coati was rapidly gaining on him. He turned off the trail, hoping that the coati would continue back the way it came, but the coati also turned and continued to pursue him. Jack placed his camera on the ground and made ready for battle. He used his polished walking stick to deliver several blows to the animal, killing him with the last blow.

Using care not to touch the dead animal, we moved it off the trail and covered its body with large stones. We were in an area often used by illegal immigrants, so we wrote "rabies" and "danger" on the stones with a permanent marker in both English and Spanish. After catching our breath, we continued on up the trail to change the film in the camera. Next to the trail and along the nearby wash, we found the tracks of this coati and marks in the sand where he had sat down and rocked back and forth.

As soon as we were in cell-tower range, we called the Arizona Game and Fish Department. No one was available to come out into the field but they assured us that we had done the right thing. Coatis rarely contract rabies, and rabies was not medically confirmed in this animal. Other diseases such as distemper can sometimes cause unusual behavior. If you encounter an animal exhibiting abnormal behavior, you should report it to the proper authorities and avoid any physical contact with the animal.

When we returned at a later date, we discovered that another animal—perhaps a gray fox or coyote—had dug under the rocks and removed the carcass. Although the rabies virus will not live long in a dead animal, it is remotely possible to contract the disease from the mucus membranes of the carcass if it is fed upon soon after death. The pile of rocks remained a warning to all those who passed.

Any animal displaying unusual behavior could potentially be suffering from rabies. Contrary to "old wives' tales," rabid animals do not always foam at the mouth. An animal that is unafraid of people may be habituated to humans from living in close proximity to them; however, this lack of fear is also a symptom of rabies. The next phase may be aggression, as displayed by this coati. All warm-blooded mammals are capable of contracting and transmitting rabies, with bats, skunks, raccoons, foxes, and coyotes being common carriers. Although the animal in the story was exhibiting classic rabid animal behavior, rabies is rare in coatis and has been confirmed in only a few isolated instances.

There are now two rabies vaccines available to humans. Anyone who handles animals, such as a veterinarian or a biologist involved in live capture of wild animals, should be vaccinated with a pre-exposure prophylaxis to prevent contracting the disease. There is no treatment for rabies after symptoms of the disease appear. If you are bitten or come in contact with the saliva from an animal suspected of having rabies, there is an effective post-exposure prophylaxis, administered in six doses over a twenty-eight-day period. Twenty years ago the shots were given in the stomach muscles and were quite painful, whereas current vaccines are relatively painless and are given in the arm.

Log on to www.cdc.gov/dvrd/rabies/prevention&control/prevent.htm for more information.

Javelina *(Pecari tacaju)*

The javelina, a salt-and-pepper-colored hoofed animal resembling a domestic hog, lives in family groups called herds or sounders. These

How many javelinas do you see in this picture? This mother is surrounded by her babies. A newborn javelina is called a "red" due to the reddish coloration of its coat, which will change to the gray of an adult as the baby matures.

groups—usually six to twelve animals, but occasionally as many as fifty—are made up of males, females, and young. Family members recognize each other by scent, from a gland located in the middle of the back just above the tail. Javelinas are omnivorous and crepuscular, meaning that they are active in the hours before and after dawn and dusk. Although the main portion of their diet consists of plants and the roots of various cacti and agaves, they also eat small mammals, snakes, and carrion. While hiking to check the cameras, we often found areas where javelinas had bedded under trees and bluffs, huddled together at night for warmth. The long, coarse, black-and-white guard hairs found in the dust of these bedding areas were a clue that they had slept there.

It appears that this neotropical species has expanded its range northward since the first Europeans arrived in the area, to as far north as the south rim of the Grand Canyon. However, it is doubtful that javelinas will ever be plentiful north of the Mogollon Rim in central Arizona due to their lack of underfur and intolerance of extreme cold weather.

Mexican brown-nosed opossum *(Didelphis virginiana californica)*

Opossum mothers carry their babies wherever they go. The babies shown at left are approximately twelve weeks old.

The Mexican brown-nosed opossum is a neotropical subspecies of the Virginia opossum (*D. v. virginiana*) found in wetter climates. Our study was the first to officially recognize a breeding population of the Mexican brown-nosed opossum in the United States—an unexpected "bonus" for us. This nocturnal omnivore—equally at home in trees and on the ground—feeds on a variety of items including insects, birds, frogs, snakes, small mammals, earthworms, fruits, berries, and carrion.

The Mexican brown-nosed opossum may be expanding its range northward. A photo taken by Don Swan in the Rincon Mountains east of

25. 2·53

Tucson is the northernmost documentation of *D. v. californica;* its range extends south through Mexico to Nicaragua. Historical records are scarce, with the earliest records of opossum in Arizona dated 1878 and 1897. It is easily differentiated from *D. v. virginiana* by its longer tail (80–90 percent of body length), greater amount (more than 30 percent) of dark coloration at the base of the tail, dark pelage on the top of the head, dark stripe through the eye, and dark legs and face.

With a gestation period of only twelve or thirteen days, females can have as many as three litters a year of twelve to twenty-five babies, each weighing

in at 1/200th of an ounce (about the size of a navy bean). Opossums are North America's only true marsupial, and in true marsupial fashion, the babies migrate immediately after birth to a pouch on the mother's stomach, where they suckle for fifty-five to sixty days. There are only thirteen teats available, and only about nine babies survive to adulthood. The next four to six weeks are spent riding on their mother's back.

White-tailed deer *(Odicileus virginianas)*

White-tailed deer are capable of bringing up one or two fawns every year. The female, or doe, cares for her fawns without help from the male, or buck. Many young prey species are born with protective coloration, including white-tailed deer, which are the main prey species for both mountain lions and jaguars.

6/24/06 6:48 AM

This white-tailed fawn's spotted coat will turn gray as it ages.

CHAPTER 5

Top Predators

It is no surprise that the top predator from the tropics is also found here.

Bobcats *(Lynx rufus)*

Bobcats, like mountain lions, raise their young without the help of the male. Both kittens and adults are spotted, which serves as protective coloration and camouflage, allowing the bobcat to remain hidden as it stalks its prey. Camouflage also enables them to hide from other predators such as the mountain lion, jaguar, coyote, fox, and great horned owl. Even adult male bobcats have been known to ambush young bobcats.

Black bear *(Ursus americanus)*

The truly omnivorous black bear eats everything—from juniper and manzanita berries, acorns, and grasses to ants, grubs, and carrion. Opportunistic feeders, bears will also catch small game, rodents, deer, javelinas, and even livestock.

16.22:29

Since they are at the top of the food chain they have little to fear from other predators.

Bear cubs are born in the den during hibernation. Even though the climate is mild in the southern Arizona sky island mountain ranges, we never photographed a bear in December, January, or February, which indicates that black bears hibernate in winter here as they do in the more northern latitudes.

Black bears mate in summer, but the sperm and egg do not unite until the timing is right for birth to take place in the den in January—a process called delayed implantation. Cubs of multiple colors can be born in the same litter (usually two cubs per litter).

In most areas of the black bears' range their color is predominantly black. In some locales they may display a white "V" on the chest and, therefore, are called "victory bears." However, in the western United States, bear colors range from black to blond, with red being the most common. Our cameras documented nearly every color phase of the "black" bear.

It must be easy for a bear to make a living, as those in the mountains of southeastern Arizona seem to have a lot of time on their hands. We photographed several that were soaking wet after taking a cooling dip in a nearby spring.

Wherever possible, we place a camera on both sides of the trail in order to document both profiles of a jaguar for purposes of identification. One camera in such a pair caught a bear (shown at left) investigating the other camera to see what fun it might provide. After getting tangled in the wires, he ripped the camera from the tree and left it lying in the trail. Somehow the camera remained functional, as attested to by the surprised expressions of two Border Patrol agents. The agents courteously replaced the camera on the tree, and it was still operating when we showed up to replace the film.

Mountain lion *(Puma concolor)*

Female mountain lions are single moms, raising their kittens without the help of a male. Look closely and you will see this mother lion (pictured to the right) suckling one of her kittens.

Kittens can be born in any month of the year, in litters of one to four. Born fully furred, with their eyes closed, they are weaned at six to eight weeks of age. When their eyes open, they are dark blue, changing to yellow as they grow older. The young lion's coat is spotted, as is the coat of the whitetail fawn, both for the purpose of protective coloration. Bears, coyotes, bobcats, and golden eagles will prey on young mountain lions. It is well known that other lions—especially adult males—will also prey on lion kittens. The female lion takes sixteen to twenty-four months to raise and condition her offspring to the point where they are self-sufficient and can fend for themselves. At the end of this period of maternal care, the female will again come into estrus and start the cycle over again.

BELOW: Two surprised Border Patrol agents.

ABOVE: Female lion and two spotted kittens.

6/03/06 10:53 PM   BJDP 52

These young mountain lions (JUST BELOW) are play-fighting to develop their motor skills as they train to become some of the top predators in North America.

The unusual photo above shows a female lion that has successfully raised a litter of four to the dispersing age of approximately eighteen months. The mother would need to kill the equivalent of three deer per week to feed a family of this size. The mortality rate for kittens by the time they reach this age is greater than 60 percent, with infanticide by adult male lions the leading cause of kitten mortality. Even the mother is sometimes killed defending her litter from a male lion. Some biologists theorize that when a female lion loses her kittens, she will soon come into estrus, as documented in African lions and domestic cats.

A male mountain lion, called a tom, has a muscular, masculine look with a head the size of a volleyball (middle left image). This can be compared to the graceful, feminine lines of a female with a head the size of a softball (lower left).

Jaguar *(Panthera onca)*

The jaguar is the largest cat in the Americas, reaching weights of over 250 pounds in South America. They range from southern Bolivia, Paraguay, and northern Argentina northward to the southwestern United States. Jaguars here at the northern limits of their range seldom weigh over 150 pounds and are similar in size to mountain lions. Males weigh 125 to 150 pounds and females 80 to 110 pounds. As we consider the number of neotropical prey species that reside in the borderlands, it is no surprise that the top predator from the tropics is also found here. This carnivore's major prey is deer and javelina, but it will take any small mammal, including skunks. The jaguar is at home in water, swims well, and can catch and eat fish and turtles.

Although the jaguar and mountain lion share a habitat (and much of the same prey), they utilize it at different times of the day. The mountain lion is crepuscular, being most active near sunrise and sunset, with some activity during midday. The jaguar, on the other hand, is almost strictly nocturnal as observed in the desert Southwest.

In southern Arizona, the jaguar was first documented in the Colorado River valley below the mouth of the Gila River by mountain man and beaver trapper James Ohio Pattie in 1827. He wrote, "We killed an animal not unlike the African leopard, which came into our camp, while we were at work upon the canoe."

From 1900 through 1995, sixty-one jaguars were documented in Arizona and New Mexico. They occurred as far north as the south rim of the Grand Canyon and at elevations ranging from 2,000 to 9,000 feet. Of these sixty-one animals, eighteen were male, seven were female, three were cubs, and the remaining thirty-three adults were unidentified as to sex. A male jaguar killed in the Dos Cabezas Mountains of southeastern Arizona in 1983 was the last jaguar documented until the two sightings in March and August of 1996, which brought the total number documented since 1900 to sixty-three.

Like mountain lions, male jaguars do not participate in the rearing of the cubs, associating with the females only during courtship and breeding. Jaguar

cubs can be born any time of the year after a gestation period of 92 to 113 days. The normal litter size is two or three cubs, each weighing twenty to thirty ounces. Their eyes open by two weeks, but the cubs may remain in their den for up to two months. By three months they eat meat almost exclusively. Like mountain lions, mother jaguars send their young off to fend for themselves at around eighteen months of age.

Although we have not yet photographed any female jaguars or their offspring, it is impossible to prove that a species or individual animal is absent or does not exist—especially in the case of an animal as secretive as the jaguar. Other biologists in the heart of the jaguars' range in Central and South America have been puzzled by the small number of females photographed by trail cameras. The best explanation is that females occupy smaller home ranges and have more restricted movements than males, thus reducing their chances of being detected.

/07   6:33 AM   B1a

CHAPTER 6

Communication

═══════

"This is my territory."

Wild animals communicate visually, vocally, and by olfactory means. These communications serve as defense mechanisms, boundary markers, means of keeping track of family members, strategies in locating a mate, or warnings for mutual avoidance. Our hidden cameras revealed many methods by which white-tailed deer, javelinas, skunks, jaguars, and mountain lions communicate.

At right, a white-tailed deer flags with its tail as it flees from a predator. Flagging, or raising the tail to expose the white hairs on the underside, is easily seen by other deer and alerts them to the possible presence of danger. This also communicates to the predator that it has been detected and that further pursuit would be futile.

The white-tailed doe and her fawn use soft bleats and rapid tail movements to communicate location, hunger, and pleasure. Javelinas grunt and squeal to keep the herd together. A spotted skunk raises its tail to warn

predators of its irritating spray (as shown above). This obnoxious liquid comes from the anal glands at the base of the tail.

The jaguar, along with the leopard, African lion, and tiger, belongs to the roaring cat family. This family of cats is grouped under the genus Panthera. According to Kevin Hansen in *Cougar: The American Lion,* "The ability to roar depends on the structure of the hyoid bone, to which the muscles of the trachea (windpipe) and larynx (voicebox) are attached." In the roaring family of cats, the hyoid bone is not attached to any other bone. Holding their heads low to the ground, both sexes use a series of guttural grunts and coughs as a means of communication over long distances, and they also utilize growls and snorts as warnings.

Mountain lions are members of the family of purring cats, grouped under the genus Felis. In this family, the hyoid bone is ossified (attached to the spine), making it possible to utter the purring sound. The bobcat, lynx, margay, ocelot, jaguarundi, and domestic cat all belong in this family.

To stay in contact, mountain lion females and cubs use mews and birdlike chirps. Females also emit a loud scream or caterwaul announcing the onset of their estrous cycle. All age groups and both sexes hiss, growl, and spit as defensive warnings.

Posturing is sometimes used in order to avoid a fight—and was vividly displayed by these adult male mountain lions caught on film below.

Scent Stations

Scent stations are a common means of communication among wild animals. These stations are both visual and olfactory signposts announcing, "This is my territory," allowing animals to tell each other who is in the neighborhood and who is looking for a date. Scent stations are also used for mutual avoidance between species and between rivals of the same species. These signposts may occur in the form of a pile of forest litter scraped into a mound—male jaguars, mountain lions, and bobcats make these "scrapes." Other signposts are scat latrines, scratch marks on a tree or fallen log, and urine sprayed on a convenient stump or fence post.

Javelinas (like the one at left) have a musk gland in the middle of the back, immediately in front of the tail, called the dorsal scent gland. They create scent markers by rubbing the musk secreted by this gland on trees or rocks in order to delineate territorial boundaries; they also use droppings as scent markers. They recognize herd members by smelling this musk. Males mark and defend their territories to maximize breeding opportunities and to protect a food source.

The adult male mountain lion uses his hind feet to make a scrape to announce his presence. He will spray the mound with urine but may or may not defecate in the area (see top photo, opposite page). Female lions will mark these scrapes with urine or scent from their facial glands (as in the middle photo to the left), allowing the male to detect the onset of their estrous cycles. The gray fox in the lower photo adds his scent to the lion scrape. Is this not the height of conceit?

Male jaguars make a scrape with their hind feet, similar to those of the lion. Occasionally there will be evidence of the animal rolling on the ground and chewing branches of shrubs in the vicinity of his scrape. Male bobcats also make scrapes, smaller than those of the lion and jaguar.

6/06/06   3:53 PM   BJDP-19N

We installed several cameras capable of recording short video clips in order to learn more about animal behaviors such as scent marking. We captured two video clips of a male jaguar scent-marking a tree to mark his territory. In one clip the jaguar is spraying the tree with urine; in the other he is claw raking and cheek rubbing.

Both bobcats and mountain lions also make scratch marks on trees and fallen logs. It was once thought that this was done to sharpen their claws and cleanse them of meat particles and blood. This may be true; however, Sue Morse, a wildlife ecologist and scent-marking expert from Vermont, has discovered another reason for this behavior. According to Sue, "What looks like mere claw sharpening is really more interesting than that. In addition to stropping his/her claws across the wood and thereby removing shards of the claws' worn keratin, this bobcat is also scent-marking. Scent-marking demonstrates a bobcat's residency in the surrounding habitat and that he/she is seeking to communicate with neighboring bobcats."

The bobcat and jaguar are shown here making scratch marks on trees.

7/25/07 7:57 PM   BJDP-JB3f

The coyote and buck (RIGHT AND BELOW) are sniffing at scent stations. The ringtail and skunk (BELOW) communicate by raising their tails.

She also notes that "The log (or upright tree branch or trunk) serves as repository for the scent secretions exuded from the interdigital glands on the bobcat's feet. As the cat intently works at shredding the wood, he or she periodically 'sniff checks' the roughened surface."

This is strikingly similar to what Sue has observed with buck deer or elk in the process of making a tree rub. The buck will repeatedly press his nose to the rub and sniff the surface he has debarked and scored with his antlers and rubbed with his forehead. In all three species—bobcat, whitetail, and elk—glandular secretions are absorbed by the frayed and abraded wood. Sue believes that the shredded wood also serves as a visual cue—calling attention to the rub. Ultimately, its real purpose is to prompt olfactory inspection of the scent messages contained therein.

"Bobcats and other felids are achieving the same result," she states. "Claw-shredded wood is not only visually conspicuous but serves as an absorbent medium in which the cat's pedal scent can be retained and olfactorily 'delivered' over time. Thus the bobcat's social status, reproductive condition, and passage through the habitat can be updated as needed and monitored by other felids in the shared environment."

The male coati (in the upper right photo) is able to judge the age of the scent left by the lion in order to avoid meeting the lion and becoming his dinner. Other animals in the forest may also check out these markers, for the same reasons as the coati.

Was the "animal behavior" exhibited by the man (lower right photo) done for the same reasons as that of the other denizens of the forest? Did he in turn leave his scent here to claim his position as the planet's top predator? Although humans have risen above this type of animal behavior, we are still an integral part of the ecosystem.

The black bear, a top predator on the study, showed very little interest in the scent markers of other animals.

CHAPTER 7

Breeding Behavior

We think this female mountain lion is looking for a date.

Peak breeding seasons can be recorded by observing when animals of opposite sexes are photographed together.

By placing cameras at these scent stations, the biologist can observe evidence of breeding behavior. Peak breeding seasons can be recorded by observing when animals of opposite sexes are photographed together, and we can calculate the time of year that young are most likely to be born by adding the gestation period of each species to the date of breeding behavior photos. Observing the dates of the actual photos of young animals allows us to test these calculations. The cameras allow us to unobtrusively make observations that we could not make any other way—such as how many different males each female is exposed to.

Documenting breeding behavior in some species, such as fox and skunk, is less reliable due to the difficulty of differentiating between the sexes by simply looking at photos. Camera-trapping projects designed to study species such as these usually target den sites to accurately record this type of behavior.

This bobcat pair is exhibiting courtship behavior.

Here, a tom and female lion engage in lion foreplay.

Hooded skunk pair.

Cottontail pairs were observed year-round.

CHAPTER 8

Who's for Dinner?

The coati is an especially sought-after delicacy.

OPPOSITE PAGE, TOP LEFT: This bobcat is carrying a cottontail rabbit. The bobcat, like the mountain lion (BOTTOM RIGHT), covers the uneaten remains of its kill and returns later to feed again. TOP RIGHT: Fox with rock squirrel. BOTTOM LEFT: Fox with white-footed woodrat.

All animals are classified as to diet. Carnivores, at the top of the food chain, eat only meat. Herbivores, at the other end of the food chain, are strictly vegetarian. Scattered throughout the food chain are the omnivores who eat both meat and plant material. The scavengers clean up the scraps left by other meat eaters and consume animals that have died from natural causes or injury. Many of the animals classified as carnivores or omnivores also depend on scavenging for a portion of their diet.

The crepuscular mountain lion, hunting during the hours just after dusk and before dawn, can kill prey much larger than itself, such as elk or mule deer. In southern Arizona their preferred prey is white-tailed deer. Lions take javelinas in limited numbers. Jack has found evidence of javelinas herding together to deter an attack by predators. As lions depend on full use of their physical abilities to make a living, they avoid the risk of being

3/04/07 8:59 PM   BJDP CALF

2/26/07 5:38 AM   BJDP CALF

injured by a group of angry javelinas. They also prey on domestic livestock. After killing its prey, the mountain lion drags the dead animal to a hidden spot under a tree or bush, where it feeds on the kill and then covers the carcass with leaves, sticks, and dirt to conceal it from scavengers. This series of photos of a lion family feeding on a calf graphically illustrates this behavior (left and above). It then retires to a safe hiding place to digest its meal and rest throughout the daylight hours. The animal will return several times until the carcass is consumed or the meat spoils. Mountain lions also feed on a wide variety of small mammals, including rabbits, rodents, skunks, porcupines, coyotes, foxes, bobcats, and even other lions. The coati is an especially sought-after delicacy.

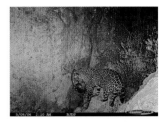

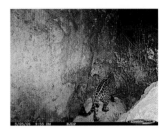

The jaguar is getting ready to dine on the unborn calf.

The jaguar's diet is much the same as the mountain lion's, although the more aggressive jaguar will take more javelinas than do mountain lions. Like the mountain lion, the jaguar drags its prey to a hidden location where it can dine in private. The jaguar, however, does not cover its kill. Although the nocturnal jaguar is most active during the darkest hours of the night, it remains with the kill night and day and guards it from scavengers. The jaguar will also scavenge animals that it did not kill. Even spoiled meat will be consumed, as attested to by this photograph of a jaguar standing on a cow that died giving birth. Although jaguars occasionally ambush and kill domestic livestock, this tendency to scavenge has caused them to be unjustly blamed in many instances. The habit of guarding its kill also makes the jaguar more vulnerable to being caught by hounds or traps.

Turkey vulture *(Cathartes aura)* and black vultures *(Coragyps atratus)*

Everyone is eventually dinner for the turkey vulture, a true scavenger that never kills its own prey but relies on its excellent olfactory receptors as well as sight to locate its meal of dead meat. We use a commercial trapping lure to entice animals to our cameras and encourage them to pose for pictures. This bait is not visible and can be located only by smell; therefore, we routinely photograph these vultures near the bait, searching in vain for a carcass.

Black vultures are also present in southern Arizona. Unable to locate their prey by smell, they often depend upon seeing turkey vultures that have landed near a carcass. The more aggressive black vultures then drive the turkey vultures away.

Other scavenging birds in the area include the crested caracara (*Polyborus plancus,* formerly *Caracara cheriway*), golden eagle (*Aguila chrysaetos*), and bald eagle (*Haliaeetus leucocephalus*).

Turkey vulture.

CHAPTER 9

Out during the Day

The motto of squirrels is
"early to bed and late to rise."

Each species is active at its own time of the day or night. Although this allows predators to hunt when their prey is most likely to be active, it also may allow the prey to be active when the predator is least likely to be active. It is all about survival. Over geologic time, each species is constantly adapting new ways of capturing prey and avoiding becoming prey. Scientists are constantly studying these complex interactions but may never completely understand them.

Scientists group animals into three daily periods of activity. Those active during the darkest hours are nocturnal. Conversely, those active during daylight hours are diurnal. Crepuscular is the term that describes activity occurring near dawn and dusk.

We plotted the daily activity patterns of all the different species captured by our cameras. Coatis, both rock and gray squirrels, and wild turkeys were found to be entirely diurnal. Cattle are also diurnal but were occasionally active in the pre-dawn hours and after sundown. Deer, javelinas, lions, coyotes, bobcats, black bears, and cottontails are crepuscular, with minor periods of activity occurring at other times of the day. Nocturnal animals include the skunk, ringtail, raccoon, gray fox, badger, opossum, and jaguar.

Coyote *(Canis latrans)*

Known as the trickster in Native American folklore, this predator depends on speed and cunning to capture prey such as cottontails and jackrabbits. This opportunistic feeder also dines on rodents, birds, frogs, carrion, and many kinds of fruit and seeds, including mesquite beans and prickly pear fruit. Primarily crepuscular, they can be active at any time of day or night.

JACK: Coyote Tale

In December of 2000, professional hunter Brandon Jones and I were down in Sonora, Mexico, trying to catch a jaguar for the purpose of attaching a radio collar. We were helping biologist Carlos López, who was studying the northernmost known breeding population of jaguars in North America. We had ten leg-hold snares set over a large area of the rugged and remote Sierra Madre mountains. Every morning we would split off in teams and check our traps.

One morning, as Brandon and I hiked into a trap site, we noticed the tracks of two coyotes in the dust of the trail, heading in the direction of the trap. They appeared to be the tracks of a male and female pair, but about fifty yards from the trap, the female had left the trail. We never saw her track again. The male, on the other hand, continued on to the trap.

When Brandon set the trap he had placed a four-inch square of canvas over the pan to keep dirt and rocks from blocking the trigger. The coyote carefully uncovered the trap and removed the canvas. Next he jumped over the trap, placed the canvas in the trail about twenty feet beyond the set, and continued on up the trail. I commented to Brandon about how smart the coyote was to detect and disable the trap so efficiently. Brandon said, "No, the smart coyote was the one that left the trail fifty yards back. The curious coyote would be easy to catch with a blind set in front of the snare."

The natural wariness of coyotes probably accounts for the low number of this species ambushed by our cameras. In order to be successful in studying wildlife, you must have a good knowledge of the target species and then design your methodology accordingly. Since we were targeting felids, it is not surprising that mountain lions, bobcats, and jaguars accounted for 16 percent of the total number of mammalian photographs. This was followed by gray fox and javelina, each at 10 percent. Only white-tailed deer were seen more often, at 23 percent.

Desert cottontail (*Sylvilagus audubonii*)

Rabbit is on the menu of every animal from snakes to raptors to jaguars. Luckily, this prolific breeder is capable of producing two or more litters of up to six hairless bunnies annually. Young rabbits are in turn able to reproduce at the early age of three months. This crepuscular herbivore dines on woody plants, grasses, and the fleshy parts of cacti such as prickly pear. Camouflage and speed are their primary means of defense.

2/21/07 8:11 AM   BJDP 52

Arizona gray squirrel *(Sciurus arizonensis)* and rock squirrel *(Spermophilus variegatus)*

A carnivore biologist's day starts before sunup and often continues long into the night. As the motto of squirrels is "early to bed and late to rise," we have concluded that a study of this diurnal animal would be a more relaxing endeavor. The shy, secretive Arizona gray squirrel is found only below the Mogollon Rim in central Arizona and in the "sky island" mountain ranges of southeastern Arizona. Its primary habitat is wooded canyons containing cottonwood, sycamore, ash, pine, oak, and walnut trees.

As we hiked along the trail, the ventriloquistic-warning whistle of the rock squirrel often accompanied us. About the size of a gray squirrel, the rock squirrel is most at home in rocky cliffs, where it dens in crevices and under rocks and boulders. Cameras set near squirrel dens soon ran out of film, as the squirrels ran back and forth busily storing food.

Cattle *(Bos taurus)*

Arizona's national forests are managed under the multiple-use concept. Seasonal livestock grazing is permitted in selected areas but is excluded from some riparian areas and other locations where threatened or endangered species might be negatively impacted. Cattle are primarily grazing animals but also eat some browse plants. Being diurnal, they have two major feeding periods—early morning and late afternoon.

Cattle and horses were first introduced to southern Arizona around 1700 by the Jesuit missionary Father Eusebio Francisco Kino and have since become a portion of the diets of large carnivores such as mountain lions, jaguars, black bears, and coyotes. According to the results of a field study conducted by Emil McCain and Colorado State University senior Matt Abbott (July 2006), remains of cattle were found in ten out of 110 lion scats collected from June 2004 to November 2005 within the BJDP study area. The majority (nine of the ten) were collected in summer months when calves are small and less able to evade predators. White-tailed deer was the primary prey item found in lion scat. Forty-three of the 110 scats analyzed contained deer remains, with deer taken equally throughout the year. Cottontail rabbit, skunk, javelina, and coati remains were next, in that order. This study indicates that in a well-balanced ecosystem, managed for diversity of species, lions prefer natural prey to introduced species, relying on livestock for prey only when natural prey numbers are low.

/06   9:07 AM   BJDP-46   Cuddeback

Gould's turkey (Meleagris gallopavo mexicana)

Wild turkeys were first documented along the present-day border of Arizona and Mexico in June 1849, when an expedition of emigrants from Texas rode through Guadalupe Pass in southeastern Arizona near San Bernardino. Benjamin Harris wrote an account of his journey, noting "several wild turkeys, some newly hatched" as they went through the pass. He also noted evidence of "several thousand wild turkeys watering in the Santa Cruz River" near the ruins of Tubac. John Bartlett of the U.S. Boundary Commission shot a "very large" turkey in Sonoita Creek upstream from its junction with the Santa Cruz River in 1851. J. Ross Browne, while traveling in southern Arizona in 1864, noted an abundance of wild turkeys on the Santa Cruz River near Tubac and also in the rolling hills in the valley between the Atascosa Mountains and the Cerro Colorado Mountains.

Wild turkeys were also chronicled along the San Pedro River as far north as the junction with the Gila by James Ohio Pattie in 1825 and by James B. Leach in 1858. These sightings, of course, were not identified as Gould's turkey, as Gould first classified them based on a specimen from Jalisco, Mexico, in 1856.

The historic distribution of the neotropical Gould's turkey appears to have been throughout the Sierra Madres in the Mexican states of Sonora, Chihuahua, and Durango, and down to the twentieth parallel in southern Mexico. North of the border, the Gould's turkey probably inhabited almost all the isolated mountain ranges in southeastern Arizona and southwestern New Mexico. Gould's turkeys may have spread naturally to these areas during less arid times, or they may have been introduced by American Indians from domesticated flocks obtained through trade with peoples in what is now Mexico before A.D. 1600.

Turkeys had largely disappeared from the southwestern United States by World War I, due to the westward expansion of white settlers. Wild Gould's were captured in Sonora, Mexico, and transplanted to the Fort Huachuca Military Reservation in the Huachuca Mountains in 1983 by the Arizona Game and Fish Department. Subsequent transplants have taken place in the

8:44 AM   BJDP 19N

Galiuro, Chiricahua, and Pinaleño Mountains. The turkey population has appeared to expand since, with turkeys being observed in the Canelo Hills, Patagonia Mountains, Babocomari River, and the Santa Rita Mountains.

During the first three years of camera trapping by the BJDP, no turkeys were photographed. In June 2004, the first turkey appeared, in the Atascosa Mountains. Since then, we have photographed several adult hens and one jake at many locations in the Atascosas. A feather collected from one of these birds identified it as a Gould's by analyzing mitochondrial DNA. These diurnal birds have expanded into this mountain range naturally, possibly from an undocumented population in northern Sonora.

The Gould's is the largest of the five subspecies of turkey found in North America, with the only other subspecies native to Arizona being the Merriam's turkey (found in the central and northern pine forests north of the Gila River). The Merriam's was transplanted to southern Arizona in the past and can still be found in small numbers in selected mountain ranges. The most notable difference between the Gould's and other turkeys is the snow-white terminal band on the tail and rump feathers. They feed on a variety of mast foods, including acorns, juniper berries, pine nuts, manzanita berries, and wild cherries. They also eat various grass seeds and insects—especially grasshoppers. They are prey to mountain lions, bobcats, hawks, and possibly golden eagles.

CHAPTER 10

Creatures of the Night

OPPOSITE PAGE (CLOSKWISE FROM TOP LEFT): The raccoon, badger, spotted skunk, and jaguar are all active at night.

Scent marking, romping, rolling on the ground, and searching for a mate are all part of the gray fox's nocturnal activities.

The animals in this chapter are almost exclusively nocturnal. With the help of the flash, which rarely seemed to bother the animals, our cameras captured a wide variety of nocturnal behavior.

Hog-nosed skunk *(Conepatus mesoleucus)*
Hooded skunk *(Mephitis macroura)*
Striped skunk *(Mephitis mephitis)*
Spotted skunk *(Spilogale gracilis)*
Camouflage is not an important means of protection for skunks as for other animals, because skunks have another means of defense. When threatened, skunks secrete a fetid liquid from their anal glands and spray it on the victim.

They sometimes stand on their front legs, raising their rumps high in the air in preparation for spraying.

Although four species of skunk are found in Arizona, we found only one early reference to skunk as we searched the historical record for any documentation of this animal in southern Arizona. The animal was referred to as a "polecat," and the location was not mentioned. We assume they were so common that most travelers and adventurers did not bother to note them in their diaries. (In Arizona, the neotropical hog-nosed and hooded skunks are at the extreme northern edge of their home range.)

The hooded skunk ranges from southeastern Arizona below the Mogollon Rim, south to northern Costa Rica. These slender-bodied, medium-sized skunks, weighing less than one kilogram (about two pounds), can be all black or black with a white-striped back. In the white-backed version, the white hairs will be mixed with black hairs. An assortment of side stripes can occur with all pelage patterns. Identifying marks include long hair on the side of the neck (the "hood"), a tail longer than the body, and a white stripe on the nose. Their diet consists of insects, fruits, small mammals, and reptiles.

Hog-nosed skunks have been found from just west of Flagstaff, Arizona, south to Nicaragua. These large, stout-bodied skunks weigh more than a kilogram (over two pounds) and are identified by their fat, naked noses; solid white backs; tails shorter than their bodies; and the lack of a stripe on their faces. They eat insects, arachnids, and fruit.

The spotted skunk is the smallest skunk, weighing less than a pound. A large round spot on the face identifies this species, which feeds almost entirely on insects.

The striped skunk feeds primarily on insects, fruits, and small mammals. One of the largest skunks, weighing more than two pounds, it has a stout body, a tail shorter than the body, a white stripe on the nose, and a black

OPPOSITE PAGE (CLOCKWISE FROM TOP LEFT): Four species of skunk are found in these borderlands: hog-nosed, hooded, spotted, and striped.

stripe on the lower back. This stripe on the lower back is not always obvious, causing them to be easily mistaken for hooded skunks.

Litters of up to four kits are born from late April to early June. Although four species of skunks share the environment during the same hours of the night, they use the habitat in different ways, thereby reducing competition. According to Christine Hass and Sheridan Stone, in a report entitled "Ecology of Hooded and Striped Skunks in Southeastern Arizona," hooded skunks den on steep hillsides, in cliffs, and in hollow trees, whereas striped skunks den in flatter ground and in sand washes. Hooded skunks prefer to forage in woodland vegetation, and striped skunks are more likely to be found in savannahs and scrub grasslands. Most of the spotted skunks captured by our cameras tended to prefer the more rocky areas in canyon bottoms. Though little is known about hog-nosed skunks, in southeastern Arizona they are found in all habitats and elevations; they appear to have a greater U.S. range than their neotropical hooded skunk cousins. They may grub for food with their large claws, but we have not learned what they eat.

Skunk is a delicacy on the lion's menu, in spite of the strong aroma and even though the nocturnal skunk is active only during the darkest hours of the night, while the crepuscular mountain lion is primarily active near dusk and dawn. During our study, we found evidence that the jaguar, which is nocturnal and active during the same hours as the skunk, also considers skunk a delicacy. Bobcats, too, have been documented preying on spotted skunks and are possible predators of the larger skunks. And coyotes and foxes have also been known to scavenge on skunk carcasses.

Ringtail (*Bassariscus astutus*)

Partially retractable claws give this catlike relative of the raccoon the ability to climb trees and bluffs in the rocky habitat it prefers. Sometimes called

"miner's cats," they were tamed and used as mousers by early-day miners. These omnivores can feed on a variety of foods, including acorns, fruit, insects, birds, small mammals, and carrion. They, in turn, are preyed upon by great horned owls, bobcats, and other carnivores. In defense, they may secrete a foul-smelling fluid from anal glands under the base of the tail. The male helps the female raise two to four young born in May or June.

Raccoon *(Procyon lotor)*

This tree-climbing night hunter is adapted to hunting in and around water. Its nimble fingers allow it to catch crayfish and minnows. With one of the most varied diets in the animal kingdom, raccoons eat fruits of all kinds, insects, worms, rodents, birds, and bird eggs, as well as carrion and household garbage. They are fierce fighters but are sometimes preyed upon by mountain lions.

Gray fox *(Urocyon cinereoargenteus)*

When we look at our photos, we are always entertained by the antics of the gray fox. He has been caught on film carrying various prey species ranging from rodents to cottontails to squirrels. This omnivore will also dine on insects and fruits of all varieties. Our photo of a gray fox climbing a one-seed juniper attests to the fact that it is a tree-climbing canid—the only one in North America. Scent marking, romping, rolling on the ground, and searching for a mate are all part of the gray fox's nocturnal activities.

Badger *(Taxidea taxus)*

The badger's preferred habitat in the Southwest is the desert floor at elevations below 3,000 feet, where the sandy soil allows it to dig for rodents and other burrowing animals—including rattlesnake. Its thick fur, loose hide, and fierce fighting ability protect it from predators, and it also exudes a foul-smelling musk. We have yet to find badger remains in any large carnivore scat.

Jaguar *(Panthera onca)*

Although the jaguar is known to be crepuscular throughout its more temperate and tropical range, here in the desert Southwest (home of the subspecies *Panthera onca arizonensis*) we found him to be strictly nocturnal. Out of a total of more than seventy nighttime photos, our cameras snapped only one jaguar in the daytime. This animal was trotting rapidly up the trail and had apparently been roused from his daytime nap.

CHAPTER 11

BJDP Jaguars

There, right before our eyes,
was jaguar #64.

One evening in January 2002, we returned from the field to find our mailbox stuffed with newly developed BJDP slides. Anticipation ran high as we looked at pictures of mountain lions, bobcats, skunks, deer, javelinas, and a host of other mammals that we routinely photographed. Some shots were devoid of any wildlife, causing us to wonder what had happened. Was the creature moving too quickly for the camera's response, was this a product of the sun heating a rock, or was the wind blowing a tree branch? One roll was almost entirely used up by a black bear playing with the camera.

Finally we came to camera site number 9, roll 7, frame 6. There, right before our eyes, was jaguar # 64—the first live, wild jaguar ever photographed in the United States by someone intentionally looking for a jaguar. The photo was taken about 6.5 kilometers north of the Mexican border, dated December 9, 2001, and showed an adult male animal approximately three years of age. For identification purposes, we now call him Macho A, *macho* being Spanish for male. You may have seen this photo, which was sent out on the wire and distributed worldwide by the Associated Press. There would be many more surprises to come, but none would ever equal the impact of that first photo.

Then on August 7, 2003, twenty months later, the same jaguar, Macho A, was photographed again at another monitoring station six kilometers farther north in the same mountain range. Both photos were of the jaguar's right profile, and the distinguishing spot patterns on the animal's right side were identical.

Macho B—the second jaguar caught by the cameras. He can be identified by the spot (circled in this photo) on his right side that looks like Pinocchio.

Can you find the spot on Macho B's left side that looks like Betty Boop?

About a year later, on August 31, 2004, a camera trap caught and photographed another adult male jaguar in the same mountain range. Spot-pattern analysis of this animal's right profile showed that this was a different animal from Macho A, and he was given the designation "Macho B."

When analyzing the spots on individual jaguars, we try to find patterns that will be easily identifiable on future photos. An unusual spot is identifiable on the right ribcage of Macho B. Look closely and you will see the long nose of cartoon character Pinocchio. Another character, Betty Boop, smiles at us from the left ribcage of Macho B. You will not find Pinocchio on Macho A's right profile.

On September 12, 2004, and on December 7, 2004, two photos were taken of the left profile of a jaguar. Betty Boop does not appear on this animal's left profile, which indicates that this animal is not Macho B. (There are no left profile photos of Macho A available for comparison.) The two photos were taken thirteen days prior to and ten weeks after the last

Macho A (THIS PAGE) and Macho B (OPPOSITE PAGE) were photographed by the same camera just under four hours apart.

identifiable photo of Macho A, so it cannot be ruled out that this unidentified animal might be Macho A.

On September 25, 2004, at 8:47 p.m., Macho A tripped one of our cameras. Then on September 26, just three hours and fifty-eight minutes later, at 12:45 a.m., the same camera at the same site filmed Macho B. Macho A has not definitely been photographed since then. As adult male jaguars are highly territorial, we do not know if Macho A was killed by Macho B or simply driven off.

Ever since the project began we had hoped to find the Baboquivari jaguar again. We heard that a trapper in the area had illegally killed a jaguar, but law-enforcement people could not verify this. It was also reported that a jaguar had been seen in the Cerro Colorado Mountains to the east of the Baboquivaris in October 1997, but we could not confirm this animal's

identity. Finally our wish came true. By comparing spot patterns on Macho B's right side, we now know that "Macho B" is our beautiful Baboquivari jaguar. Macho B has remained in the area of the study, crossing back and forth between Arizona and Sonora. We have subsequently photographed him over fifty times, as of July 2007.

To sum up, the Borderlands Jaguar Detection Project has documented two adult male jaguars and a possible third individual in southeastern Arizona from March 2001 to July 2007. On February 19, 2006, lion hunters Warner Glenn and Kelly Glenn Kimbro bayed another adult male jaguar in the bootheel region of New Mexico. Spot-pattern analysis of this animal's left and right profiles shows that this is a new animal, photographed for the first time. This latest sighting brings the total number of jaguars documented in Arizona and New Mexico since 1900 to sixty-five.

Along the Way

People probably startled us more than did an occasional deer, snake, or exotic bird.

We saw many raptors, including golden eagles, Cooper's hawks, gray hawks, zone-tail hawks, prairie falcons, peregrine falcons, and kestrels. We studied our bird books and became more skilled at identifying these magnificent birds.Once while we hiked up a remote canyon, a dark-colored hawk flew over us. It led us up the canyon and landed in the top of a tall tree ahead of us, making a shrill call as it flew. It then left the tree and flew high, mingling with two turkey vultures soaring overhead. We noticed that the vultures and the hawk looked very similar in flight, and we later learned that this hawk mimics the vulture in order to hide from its intended prey. A light band on this particular hawk's tail feathers confirmed that it was a zone-tailed hawk. Six weeks later, we saw it again in the same spot and decided it must be guarding a nest nearby.

Another morning as we drove to a trailhead, a Cooper's hawk flew across our path, dangling a young cottontail from its talons. We stopped and watched as the hawk landed at the foot of a nearby tree, turning its head back and forth, searching the sky for competitors. It was not intimidated by our truck, and Jack was able to video the bird for several minutes. Finally we drove away, allowing it to enjoy its breakfast.

In the warmer months we often heard the elegant trogon (*Trogon elegans*) as it foraged in the mid-level forest. Sometimes called the "coppery-tailed trogon," this large bird inhabits the mountains of southeastern Arizona in the summer and returns to Mexico in the winter. Shy and elusive, these tropical birds are difficult to spot among the lush foliage in the rugged canyons near the border. Though we often had heard them call, we had never had more than a fleeting glimpse of one. One day as we hiked in an area close to one of our cameras, we heard a trogon calling in the distance. We changed film and batteries in the camera, then sat down to eat our lunch. We perched on large flat rocks with binoculars ready and listened as the "seal bark" call came closer. Suddenly the trogon landed approximately fifty feet from us and, to our amazement and delight, remained in the same spot long enough for us to observe its breast: crimson at the bottom with a white stripe and dark green above this. It eventually flew down the canyon but later returned and posed in the same large sycamore tree as before, this time giving us a view of its metallic green back and coppery tail shimmering in the leafy backdrop. As it sat there croaking, it turned its head to and fro and gave us a profile view of its eyes and beak. What an unexpected bonus to the day—and a memory for the days to come!

In contrast to the evasive trogon, a pair of painted redstarts boldly ate and drank only a few feet away from us at a spring where water dripped into an enclosure. Wild vines covered the spring, and the birds seemed oblivious to us as they darted in and out of the leaves. Summer tanager, acorn woodpecker, cardinal, phainopepla, yellow-billed cuckoo, and pyrrhuloxia are some of the more striking and interesting birds that surprised us and brightened our days.

We tried to keep our eyes on the trail in spite of the bird distractions overhead. We were constantly aware of the danger of stepping on or startling a rattlesnake, yet we surely passed many snakes without being aware of their presence. Twice our mules "told" us there was a rattler nearby—they always seemed to sense their presence before we did. Anna watched Jack and his mule perform some rodeo tricks the time a rattler "buzzed" close to the road we were traveling.

Another time, in a different mountain range, we found what appeared to be a slender vine draped on a branch of a tree at the side of the trail near the dry stream bottom. Upon closer examination, it proved to be a small snake

Fresh mountain lion tracks.

with a long snout and a black eye stripe, basking in the warm afternoon sun. We picked it up, recorded it on our video cameras, and gently placed it back in the tree. We later learned that it was a rare and mildly venomous vine snake. Vine snakes prey upon lizards, often catching them on the ground. These neotropical snakes range from five miles north of the Mexican border in the Pajarito Mountains of southern Arizona to their southernmost limit in Brazil.

Jack traced and photographed animal tracks that were clear and fresh while Anna entered them as data in the Palm Pilot. Most tracks appeared across our path and soon disappeared, but once we found a very clear, fresh set of tracks belonging to a female lion. We followed these distinct tracks the entire one-mile length of the transect. When the lion had neared the camera, she made a detour around the camera tree and continued up the wash. Though we did not photograph this lion, she taught us something about lion behavior. Maybe she had watched us from a bluff as we changed film and batteries in the camera that she carefully avoided. After following her tracks for such a long distance, Anna found it much easier to distinguish a lion track from that of a canid.

We found evidence of several lion kills. The lion usually drags the animal to a spot under a tree and then covers the kill with leaves and branches. This allows the lion to eat, leave the kill, and then return to eat more. Twice we found drag marks in the dirt and followed them to the kill, and in both instances the prey was a white-tailed deer. We also discovered the complete skeleton of a lion, which we collected to be used for educational purposes.

People We Met along the Trail

People probably startled us more than did an occasional deer, snake, or exotic bird. With the exception of hunters during certain seasons, we didn't expect to see many other humans on these remote trails.

The Border Patrol agents we met were friendly and helpful. Many of the transects lie along trails used by illegal border crossers and drug smugglers, and though we rarely met any of these, we found evidence of their presence—abandoned cans of food, empty water containers, rotting bedrolls and clothing, tons of trash, and even discarded diapers and cans of baby formula.

We met several cowboys along the trail. Two come to mind, both colorful and interesting. One has replaced his trusty *caballo* (horse) with an ATV 4-wheeler, which allows him to easily check fences, cattle, and the general condition of the ranch. He enjoys buzzing up and down the rough and dusty roads, and he always stopped to chat with us as we rode our mules to one of the more remote cameras. He was always ready to tell us his latest woes, which ranged from cut fences to trashed waterholes, or gates that were left open or shut, as the case might be. The old rule of "leave the gate the way you found it" seems to be unknown, forgotten, or ignored by many who travel through these ranches today.

ANNA: Track Discovery

One momentous track discovery began while we embarked on a shopping trip in Tucson. Jack was trying on a straw hat at a local Western store when his cell phone rang. I heard him say, "Are you sure?" and then, "We'll be there as soon as we can."

BJDP biologist Emil McCain and his father, Jim, were hiking to a camera site in the study area when they came to a stock pond and discovered fresh tracks leading to the edge of the pond. The footprints were clear and undisturbed in the mud surrounding the water. The McCains were sure that they were looking at jaguar tracks.

We bought the hat and were out the door, forgetting the other items on our "to do in town" list. After a quick stop at the hardware store to purchase plaster of paris, we headed south to meet the McCains, who were waiting for us on a ridgetop in the shade of an oak tree. We parked the truck and hiked to the pond. It was a warm June day with a slight breeze. Small, fluffy clouds floated overhead and reflected in the muddy water. And there were the tracks, large and distinct in the mud: the first jaguar tracks documented in the study.

Emil and Jim had already measured and photographed the tracks. We turned the job of casting the tracks over to Jim, a professional sculptor. He knew how to mix the plaster to the perfect consistency, how to pour it into the mold, and when to remove the mold from the cool, wet track in the mud. We watched him work, learned from this expert, and tried to contain our excitement. When it was safe to brush the sand and debris from the hardened plaster, he lifted the fragile mold out of the incredibly clear track. We carefully placed this in the truck inside a box lined with dry desert grass to help cushion it from the bumps and jolts on the ride back to the ranch.

Several months later, Jim presented us with a bronze jaguar track that he had made using a process called the "lost wax" method. He also made tracks cast in plaster that we sold to raise funds for the camera project. Our bronze track is a treasure, beautiful to touch and behold and a reminder of that memorable June day.

Another wonderful *vaquero* (cowboy) works for a large ranch in the study area. He has lived in this area many years and knows the country and the animals that live there, as well as the native plants and their uses. One day we found him waiting for some other vaqueros who were out looking for stray calves. Meanwhile, his horse was tied to a tree, and he passed the time picking wild oregano in a flat meadow between the wash and the road. He told us in Spanish that this herb is very good dried and sprinkled on foods, especially on *pescado,* or fish.

We have worked with several ranchers in the study area, and their help has been invaluable. They give us permission to pass through private land, and one ranch even allows Emil to set up his headquarters in an empty ranch house. This benefits the project as well as the rancher, as Emil's presence helps safeguard the house and surrounding buildings in this remote area. And he can more easily access the camera and transects while living in the "backyard" of the study area.

Jack spoke to several cattle and land management groups at the headquarters of this ranch. All these groups were eager to learn about the jaguar as well as the other wildlife species that share space with the cattle and the cowboys.

JACK: Injured Traveler

Working alone one wintry day in January, I parked the truck at the end of the road and was eating lunch before hiking the mile and a half into one of the camera sites when I looked down the canyon and saw a man walking slowly and painfully toward the truck. He was using two sotol stalks for crutches and his right ankle was in a splint made from short pieces of the same plant. Upon reaching the truck, he said in Spanish that his ankle was broken and that his group had left him and gone on. I gave him food and water and asked him to wait at the truck while I completed my work. Two hours later the man was still there and I took him to a main road and flagged down a passing Border Patrol vehicle. The two agents questioned the man in Spanish and found out he was from Magdalena, Sonora, about sixty miles south of the U.S.-Mexico border. They lifted the man's coat collar and showed me the fibers from a burlap bag imbedded in the fabric of his jacket. Over the years, our cameras photographed a large amount of smuggling activity, so I knew that many of the bales of marijuana are wrapped in homemade packs made from burlap bags. This man was obviously not coming to America to seek a better way of life.

We find these ranchers to be excellent stewards and caretakers of the land they share with the elusive jaguar, and to cooperate well with the various governmental land-management agencies. The rancher has a huge investment in the land, and it is to his benefit—as well as that of the jaguar—that they use good land-management techniques on their shared space.

Arizona is one of the fastest-growing states in the nation; as the influx of people fuels the demand for housing, private lands are being developed at an alarming rate. Much of this private land, currently owned by the livestock industry, is being grazed in conjunction with the adjacent federal- and state-controlled lands. As land values rise, property taxes increase proportionately, creating a temptation (and sometimes a necessity) to sell these lands to developers. Southern Arizona is made up of many isolated mountain ranges surrounded by broad valleys. The mountains are primarily owned by the United States Forest Service. The valleys are a mix of state and privately owned lands, and lands managed by the BLM. Wildlife, especially large carnivores, need travel corridors across the valleys to maintain connectivity between the mountain ranges. By isolating these ranges, we not only inhibit the genetic diversity of a species, we risk losing entire species when local catastrophes such as fire, drought, or disease affect local populations. Natural recovery and recolonization become impossible as our valleys fill up with people. Without the open space of the ranches, there would almost certainly be no jaguars in the U.S.

5/05/06   7:08 PM   BJDP-46

CHAPTER 13

Don't Look Now, You're on Hidden Camera!

Our cameras "ambushed" whoever
and whatever passed in front
of the lens.

Our cameras are placed in strategic locations along trails near the Mexican border. Our goal is to make these camera sites as non-intrusive as possible along trails with a strong possibility of animal activity, in hopes of capturing images of four-legged critters going about their daily business. However, many two-legged varieties have also been "ambushed" by our cameras.

In the early days of the study, Jack hiked to a remote ridgetop to collect the first roll of film from this site. There he found a large rock blocking the camera lens. He took this for a warning that someone did not want to be photographed on this ridge. He then moved the camera to a more secluded spot. When the film was developed, the first picture revealed a male mountain lion, the next a curious roadrunner, and the third and last … two very startled drug smugglers staring at the camera. We have since installed signs in Spanish

and English explaining that the cameras are for wildlife research. We have had some problems with vandalism, but not enough to severely impact the project. Two cameras were stolen, and since they were chained and locked to trees, a lot of effort went into cutting all the branches from a juniper and lifting the camera over the top. Several cameras were smashed with rocks. We don't know who did this, but we doubt that illegal entrants were responsible for all of the vandalism.

The five-strand barbed-wire border fence that stands between most of the United States and Mexico is not much of a deterrent to illegal immigration. This fence has been cut in so many places that it no longer prevents free-ranging livestock from crossing from one side of the border to the other. A solid barrier fence, more commonly called "the border wall," of sufficient height may make it more difficult for people to cross and would certainly stop livestock from straying over the line. Such a fence, however, would be a catastrophic barrier to wildlife travel corridors.

Wild animals have no concept of international borders and have been traveling freely for thousands of years. Large carnivores, such as jaguars, lions, bobcats, black bears, and wolves occupy large home ranges in order to utilize the available prey base without reducing their food supply. Our apparently resident jaguar occupies a home range encompassing more than 500 square miles in Arizona alone. He has been photographed many times within fifty yards of the international border, so we can reasonably assume that a part of his home range lies in Mexico. Leading jaguar biologists theorize that our Arizona jaguars could be immigrant males from a core population located 135 miles south of Douglas, Arizona, in Sonora, Mexico. Are these immigrants vital to the breeding population in Mexico? This is one of the questions we are attempting to answer.

Many people with a wide variety of interests and activities utilize our national forests. Visitors to our sites included backpackers, hunters, cowboys, undocumented immigrants, Border Patrol agents, bird-watchers, and hikers (individuals as well as large groups on organized tours). Our cameras "ambushed" whoever or whatever passed in front of the lens. Some are aware of the cameras and some are not. One hiker walked past the camera unaware of its presence, but by the time the next frame was shot, the same hiker leaped in front of the lens, and we have a good close-up of him making a face at the camera. It's always fun to see the pictures of people photographing our cameras or crawling on all fours in front of the camera, pretending to be a bear or large cat.

In the bottom of a particularly brushy and thorny canyon we captured the image of a totally nude male. All he wore were his tennis shoes. We always wore long denim pants and long-sleeved shirts as protective clothing when we walked the transects. Our nude hiker must have suffered a few "cat claw" scratches in some tender areas as he strolled through the brush. A couple of

This immigrant family was photographed after dark on Christmas Eve, miles from the nearest road.

months after the nude hiker picture, we got our second jaguar photo. In the early days of the project, each jaguar photo was followed by a press release, and the story would instantly go out worldwide. As the phone rang nonstop with requests for interviews after the first jaguar photo release, Jack had learned his lesson. So on this second occasion, he loaded up two mules in the gooseneck and went on an extended pack trip, while Anna stayed home to answer the phone and deal with reporters. One interviewer asked if we ever captured any unusual shots on our cameras. Of course, Anna mentioned the nude hiker. Guess what was published in the paper? We often wondered how many people read the article and thought, "I wonder if that was me?"

Obviously, as was the case with the Mexican brown-nosed opossum and the Gould's turkey, we never expected to capture this rare photograph. We named this new species *Homo erectus denudo*. It is common for research projects to reveal unanticipated secrets. These surprises sometimes solve long-hidden mysteries, but more often they lead to unanswered questions. Our photo log now contains four pictures of people hiking in the nude in the Coronado National Forest. As near as we can tell, the cameras have ambushed two different males of the species we now call *H. e. denudo*. What other secrets would be revealed about this species? Are these lone males dispersing from a faraway population, or are they part of a so-far-undiscovered breeding population within the borders of the national forest? Why have we not photographed any females? What are their numbers and what can we learn of their social behavior? We are forever hopeful that future photos will "reveal" answers to these questions.

The majority of people engaged in recreational activities were photographed in the more popular and easily accessed areas of the forest. Illegal activity was confined to the more remote areas and took place primarily at night. Recreational and occupational use accounted for 60

Cuddeback Digital Camera 11/29/05 4:55 PM BJDP 50

percent of the human activity, and illegal activity accounted for 40 percent.

Does this human activity have an impact on the daily activity of the jaguar? We don't know. As jaguars are almost strictly nocturnal, it is doubtful that recreational use at its current level has much impact, although nocturnal human activity such as drug or human smuggling could certainly interrupt a jaguar's nightly travels.

CHAPTER 14

Fire and Water

OPPOSITE PAGE: Vegetation is damaged by a fire, but wildlife is present shortly afterward.

Under drought conditions, a portion of the forest floor is covered with highly flammable dead grasses left over from wetter times.

Many of our rancher friends have a standard greeting: "Howdy! It's good to see you. Have you had any rain?" We each moved to Arizona as young children—Jack from Iowa, and Anna from Nevada and New Mexico—and grew up in the Sonoran Desert. We know how important water and rainfall are to the people, animals, and plants that make the desert their home. In Ray, Arizona, Anna remembers never letting a faucet run, and catching water in a pan in the sink, then reusing every droplet that was caught.

Since 1996 (before our study began in 2001), Arizona has experienced one of the most prolonged droughts in recorded history. At times the oak trees shed their leaves to preserve precious moisture stored within the plant, and then the oak-covered hillsides look like a forest of dead trees. When

summer rains actually do occur, they miraculously restore the trees to their former vigor. It is not known at this time how this drought will affect the health of the forest over the long term. Could we see the oaks retreating to the wetter canyon bottoms, leaving the ridges a sea of grasses?

Meanwhile the drought continues. Under drought conditions, a portion of the forest floor is covered with highly flammable dead grasses left over from wetter times. Manzanita shrubs die, and oaks and other trees shut down to conserve precious moisture. This increased fuel load is highly susceptible to wildfire, especially from April through July, before the monsoon rain typically arrives.

Such a fire occurred in our study area in April 2002, burning approximately 1,200 acres. One of our cameras in the center of the fire was able to record the smoke and flames. Even though its case was badly melted, the camera

A whitetail doe moves through a fire-ravaged landscape.

functioned throughout the event and even recorded a whitetail doe moving through the smoke and ashes after the fire had passed.

When we returned to remove and replace the damaged camera, we were amazed at how quickly the land had begun to heal itself. Everywhere we looked, tiny green shoots burst forth out of the charred earth. Six weeks later the tiny shoots were small plants, some with miniature pink blossoms.

Fire is a naturally occurring event and can be good for the overall health of the ecosystem. Fortunately, the summer rains were good that year, and grasses and other browse plants flourished. The replacement camera continued to monitor wildlife movement as the area recovered. Wildlife detections were fewer for a short time, but deer soon utilized the area again. As the plant life rapidly recovered, deer numbers appeared to increase. Small mammals such as skunks, coatis, and foxes showed a sharp decrease over the next year or so. Although lion sign was abundant outside the burned area, few lions were detected within the burned area. The absence of overhead cover may have made it difficult for mountain lions to remain hidden while stalking their prey. After a couple of years, as the plant life rapidly recovered, detections of lions and small mammals also increased.

The trail to the camera site winds through a large stand of velvet-pod mimosa (*Mimosa dysocarpa*). Though blackened by the fire, this tenacious, spiny shrub recovered quickly. A year after the fire, its bright green primary and secondary leaflets, with pink flower spikes at the ends of the stems, covered the burned area. The mimosa appeared to be healthier and more vigorous than before the fire. We had to cut away some of the branches that reached across the trail in order to pass through on the mules. The grass was so high we had difficulty even finding the trail at first!

Engelmann's prickly pear (*Opuntia engelmannii*) is abundant in the area, and some of the cactus pads were burned beyond hope of recovery. Others, though singed, put on new growth (small green pads) and bloomed profusely the next spring. Another plant that persisted after the burn was the coral bean (*Erythrina flabelliformis*), whose showy red blossoms waved in the spring wind, oblivious to the effects of the smoke and flame. It would be interesting to know how much heat its tough red seeds can withstand.

Wild animals are naturally attracted to water; therefore, many of our cameras are located near sources of this precious resource. As we checked the cameras, we also recorded data regarding the nearby spring, pool, or stream, whose conditions changed with the season and amount of annual rainfall. During a particularly wet summer, water flowed through the length of one particular canyon, although this transect was normally dry. At one end of the canyon, we found a large, deep hole filled with water. It was summer and our

Mountain lions (THIS PAGE) and children (OPPOSITE PAGE) alike enjoy a pool of water.

grandchildren were visiting us, so we brought them there to swim. The hole was deep and wide enough for them to jump into from the large rock next to the swimming hole. It was definitely a "kids' paradise," and we spent the day there making memories. These grandchildren are all in high school now, but they still talk about that day they went swimming in the canyon "water hole." Yet when we returned the following summer we found the same hole completely dry and filled with sand, with only small pockets of water left in the stream above.

As the study progresses, we continually realize that this is much more than an absence/presence search for the jaguar. As we walk the trails, collect data, look at slides, encounter wildlife, meet new and interesting people, and soak in the beauty of the canyons and mountains, we are reminded that we have only just begun. Our August 1996 discovery continues to lead us to new horizons and vistas.

ANNA: Wildflowers

—

We checked the cameras every six weeks, and this rotation meant we monitored them at a slightly different time each month and year. I kept a written record of our excursions. In these journals I recorded thoughts, impressions, anecdotes, and most important—wildflowers.

Early in our marriage, Jack learned to brake for wildflowers. "Mariposas!" was synonymous with "Stop now!" As we hiked or rode the mules to a camera site, the flowers along the way were a wonderful, unexpected bonus. Stopping a mule on a trail is much easier than stopping a 4-wheel-drive truck whizzing down the road. We hiked through, around, and over flowers. While looking for sign of large cats we often took "flower breaks."

We found many familiar friends, such as larkspur (*Delphinium scaposum*), Arizona poppy or caltrop (*Kallstroemia grandiflora*), Mexican gold poppy (*Eschscholtzia mexicana*), prickly poppy (*Argemone platyceras*), Goodding's verbena (*Verbena gooddingii*), Parry's penstemon (*Penstemon parryi*), chuparosa (*Justicia californica*), mariposa lily (*Calochortus kennedyi*), and fairy duster (*Calliandra eriophylla*). Mariposa lilies bloomed profusely on dry, barren hillsides, while several varieties of penstemon grew higher than our waists along remote canyon trails.

We were startled by the surprising, intense color of the coral bean flower. These flaming red blossoms bloom on the bare stalks of the plant before the foliage appears. Later the blossoms become large green pods that eventually turn brown and split open to reveal the bright red, extremely poisonous coral bean. Coral bean, or chilicote, as it is sometimes called, grows profusely on several areas of the study.

We wore out pages in our wildflower books as we searched for the names of unfamiliar flowers and plants. We discovered that it is necessary to own several books on wildflowers in order to track down some of these mysterious flora. I often went to the library and checked out additional books when our own books left us still seeking a correct name.

Coral bells (*Heuchera sanguinea*) greeted us year-round. They are known to flower from March through October. Clinging bravely to steep, rocky ledges, these plants grow in small crevices in the rocks. The rounded, reddish-green leaves of the plant remained even in the coldest months of the year. We found them growing in the same location each time we hiked certain transects.

Many years ago, we found an *Amoreuxia plamatifida* plant in the Sierrita Mountains. Commonly called Mexican yellowshow, this plant is also known by its Seri name, *saiya*. It has leaves shaped like palm leaves, with large flowers containing five bright yellow petals, four of which have a reddish color in the center, and its roots were a food source for some Native Americans. We continued to search for saiya, assuming that it was a rare species. Then one July, as we hiked our transects during the monsoon season, we discovered not one or two but thousands of these gold-colored plants, covering a hillside. We were overwhelmed with the beauty and abundance of the "rare" plant we had searched for all these years; it was

another treasure, an unexpected gift, and we found the saiya growing within two miles of the spot where we recorded the first jaguar tracks. We wondered if our jaguar may have padded silently through these exotic flowers on a dark, starry night.

CHAPTER 15

Conservation Efforts

Not only is the jaguar an endangered
species, but it is rarely found at
the northern limits of its range.

It is an understatement to say that jaguar conservation is vital. Not only is
the jaguar an endangered species, but it is rarely found at the northern limits
of its range. Fortunately, the number of individuals and groups involved in
the conservation movement is increasing, both in the United States and in
Mexico, where at an international conference, 2005 was proclaimed the Year
of the Jaguar.

In comparison, during the mid to late 1930s through the 1940s, the Lee
Brothers—well-known professional hunters from southeastern Arizona—
hunted jaguars in several areas of Mexico, from Sonora south to the state of
Nayarit. Dale Lee, the youngest brother, was the most avid jaguar hunter of
the family. Jack knew Dale and hunted with him several times during the last
years of his career (he passed away in 1986 at age seventy-eight). Dale was a

great storyteller, and Jack spent many hours around a campfire listening to his tales. In his sixty years as a professional hunter, Dale never saw any sign of jaguar in the United States. We wish he could have lived long enough to witness this renewed interest and effort on the jaguar's behalf.

In 1997, we met two prominent researchers at a jaguar conservation meeting. Dr. Carlos López González, a biologist from Mexico City, and David E. Brown, a professor at Arizona State University, were documenting jaguar occurrences in Mexico and the southwestern United States. They researched historical records and conducted firsthand interviews with individuals in Sonora, Chihuahua, and the U.S.

When we became involved in jaguar conservation following our 1996 jaguar encounter, Jack reread Dale Lee's book, *Life of the Greatest Guide,* and listened to audiotapes about his adventures. Using information from Dale's book and tapes, Jack plotted the three areas where Dale had found jaguars in Mexico in the 1930s and 40s—in the swamps of Nayarit, on the west coast of Sinaloa near Dimas, and at the junction of the Río Aros and Río Bavispe at the headwaters of the Río Yaqui in Sonora (an area known as Tres Ríos). Jack shared this information with researchers Carlos and Dave.

Northern Jaguar Project Carlos and Dave went to this Tres Ríos area north of the village of Sahuaripa in Sonora and located the northernmost known breeding population of jaguars in North America—just a short 135 miles south of the twin cities of Douglas, Arizona, and Agua Prieta, Sonora. Some scientists hypothesize that the jaguars recently documented in southern Arizona and New Mexico are immigrants from this population. Carlos began a jaguar study at Tres Ríos that led to the formation of the Northern Jaguar Project in 2003—a cross-border group dedicated to research and conservation.

Carlos and Dave published the results of their study in the book *Borderland Jaguars/Tigres de la Frontera*. Their work in the Tres Ríos area, and also along the natural corridors that lead from Mexico to the United States, is valuable to jaguar conservation.

The Northern Jaguar Project later joined forces with Naturalia, a Mexican environmental organization based in Mexico City, and purchased 10,000 acres to form the Northern Jaguar Reserve in the Los Pavos sanctuary (in the Tres Ríos area). They also own the adjacent 30,000 acres, knowing that this area contains the northernmost documented breeding population of jaguars. This is also the northernmost breeding ground for the military macaw and the river otter, and home to one of the southernmost populations of bald eagle.

Valdez/Rosas Jaguar Study To the north and east of the Northern Jaguar Reserve and across the Río Aros, Octavio Rosas Rosas, under the guidance of wildlife professor Dr. Raúl Valdez of New Mexico State University in Las Cruces, conducted a jaguar study. Octavio earned his doctoral degree by collecting biological information and looking at jaguar-human relationships, in particular ranchers' reactions when jaguars killed livestock.

Octavio discussed this situation with two hunter/biologists from the United States during a capture effort. One evening around the campfire, they conceived the idea of establishing an association of area ranches that would benefit financially from the wildlife resources found on their properties. Ranchers would receive financial incentives in exchange for not killing jaguars depredating their livestock.

Octavio met with landowners. He also held a three-day session with schoolchildren and residents of Nácori Chico, where he had the difficult task of emphasizing the value of wildlife conservation. One night, a mountain lion attacked a teenage boy while he and his father were camped near the town. The father saved his son by killing the lion, using an axe in hand-to-claw combat. Severely injured, the young man would need extensive plastic surgery. Octavio was asked to come and discuss this event with the townspeople. Upon arrival, he discovered that the offending lion's carcass had been dragged around town and then burned. The people told him that any jaguars in the area would meet the same fate.

Still, Octavio persisted in his task of educating the people. He eventually gained a respect rarely shown to a carnivore biologist—especially significant in a region where beef rules and large carnivores attack children. In 2003, he established the Programa de Conservación de Jaguar en la Sierra Alta de Sonora, an official unit recognized by the Mexican government. In Mexico, this type of program is known as "UMA," also known as Unidades de Manejo para la Conservación de la Vida Silvestre (roughly translated as Management Units for Conservation of Wildlife). There are now ten ranchers and a plan to add three more ranches to this UMA, for a total of 120,000 acres under conservation agreement and jaguar protection. Ranchers have agreed to sustain livestock loss to jaguars in exchange for tourists being allowed to visit their properties with the possibility of sighting a jaguar.

Primero Conservation Outfitters began in 2004 to bring both ecotourists and conservation-minded hunters to the ranches participating in the UMA. During the first year, twenty hunters and twenty ecotourists and students visited the conservation area, and by 2008, participating ranchers should receive approximately $118,000 as a direct financial return.

"Big cat habitat" such as this is being cared for by livestock operators under the watchful eye of our governmental land-management agencies.

The Malpai Borderlands Group, mentioned in Chapter 2, is actively purchasing "conservation easements" from area ranchers in southeastern Arizona and southwestern New Mexico. These place encumbrances on deeds to the protected land, prohibiting commercial development. The contracts also prohibit human-caused degradation of the range and its wildlife. By 2007, the Malpai Borderlands Group had purchased easements on more than 75,000 acres of private lands. The Nature Conservancy also holds conservation easements on 235,000 acres of private ranchlands in southwestern New Mexico. If you add in the neighboring 134,620 acres of federal- and state-leased grazing lands, it amounts to 445,380 acres in which the jaguar is free to roam.

Another ranch-community-based conservation group, the **Altar Valley Conservation Alliance,** is working to restore wildlife habitat in the 500,000-

acre Altar Valley west of Tucson. The valley has experienced severe erosion over the past hundred years, and the alliance is organizing a restoration program to improve watershed and habitat conditions through prescribed burning, innovative conservation practices, and sustainable grazing.

To prevent fragmentation of the valley, the alliance is cooperating with Pima County to protect land under the Sonoran Desert Conservation Plan, protecting more than 46,000 acres of private land and grazing leases in the Altar Valley. The alliance has also entered into an innovative "conservation bank" agreement with a local ranch owner and the U.S. Fish and Wildlife Service.

Sky Island Alliance, an environmental group based in Tucson, Arizona, recently began a jaguar study utilizing camera traps in Sonora, south of the BJDP area. We eagerly await the results of this new study.

The information generated by these research projects is vital for jaguar conservation. Tropical lowlands make up most of the jaguar habitat throughout its range. Historically, here in the north, jaguars have been found from the Sonoran Desert at sea level to the subalpine forests of central Arizona and New Mexico at elevations over 9,000 feet. Very little is known about the habitat requirements and ecological dynamics of this subspecies of jaguar known as *Panthera onca arizonensis* (the Arizonan jaguar). We urge all of the biologists conducting these studies to make publication of their data a number-one priority. We need this information now, in order that sensible, science-based decisions can be made to protect this small population of jaguars.

At the May 3, 2007, meeting of the Arizona-New Mexico Jaguar Conservation Team, held in Douglas, Arizona, we were honored to hear from two renowned cat researchers. Dr. Eric Gese (USDA/Wildlife Services/ National Wildlife Research Center, Department of Wildland Resources, Utah State University) discussed the results of a jaguar depredation study conducted by Sandra Cavalcanti (PhD candidate, Department of Wildland Resources, Utah State University) in the Pantanal area of Brazil. Sue Morse, a wildlife ecologist from Vermont, founded Keeping Track, an organization that trains citizen scientists to document evidence of wildlife movements within areas of possible future development. She presented a slide show on Canada lynx research. As a member of the jag team's research committee, she compared the lynx research along the Canadian border with our borderland jaguar research. Both Eric and Sue pointed out the value of utilizing GPS radio telemetry and radio collars when studying wide-ranging carnivores. Both researchers emphasized the large amount of data that radio telemetry would provide that traditional, non-invasive study methods such as track transects and camera traps could not reveal. The jag team is considering the initiation of such a study.

CHAPTER 16

Past, Present, and Future

I look at the condition of the land today
as compared to what I saw in the 1950s, and
my eyes truly see a pristine landscape.

JACK: Reflections

Over the years I have conducted more than fifty slide shows and video presentations entitled "On the Trail of the Jaguar." Some of these shows were arranged through the jag team's educational outreach program and have reached a wide array of organizations, some of which could be described as activist groups with specific agendas. These did not always agree with the aims and goals of the jag team or the Borderlands Jaguar Detection Project, but no organization's request for a presentation was refused. I am sure that some groups were skeptical about a lion hunter conducting a wildlife study on the conservation of large carnivores, yet I note that all groups received me courteously. Each show was followed by a question and comment session.

Typically this portion of the program lasted longer than the slide show, and I was often taken to task over a comment I made in the narration of the video. While showing film clips of the majestic scenery in the Coronado National Forest, I stated, "I tip my hat to the wildlife and range managers employed by the various land-management agencies that keep a watchful eye on these pristine lands. I also want to express a word of thanks to the ranchers whose animal husbandry practices help maintain these range lands and help to keep them attractive to wildlife."

The word "pristine" starts the questioning. In *Webster's New World Dictionary,* "pristine" is defined as "1. Characteristic of the earliest or an earlier period or condition; original. 2. Still pure or untouched; uncorrupted; unspoiled." I concede that according to this definition it would be hard to find any such place on the planet. If you go back to the "earliest period," the area would have to be at the bottom of a primitive sea in order to be pristine. "Untouched; uncorrupted; unspoiled"? Hardly. The "original condition" is also difficult to define. Do we use as our standard the era before the 1500s, when Europeans first arrived in North America, or do we go back ten or fifteen thousand years "or more"—archaeologists are thinking even earlier, apparently—to the time when man first crossed the Bering Sea? We can never hope to fully restore our national forests to any of these conditions. We can, however, strive to improve and maintain them to the best of our abilities.

Spain was the first European country to explore and settle what is now the southwestern United States and northern Mexico—an area they called the Pimería Alta. Father Eusebio Kino introduced livestock to the area around 1700. Livestock numbers increased throughout the 1800s as settlers from the East occupied the land. Forage appeared to be unlimited, and the number of cattle grazing on this forage soon exceeded the carrying capacity of the open range. Several periods of drought from 1885 through the early

1900s, punctuated intermittently by El Niño flooding during the early twentieth century, eroded the landscape and created a catastrophic condition.

In 1951, when I was nine years old, my dad introduced me to camping, hunting, and fishing in our national forests. Our forest lands were on the road to recovery at this time, although the degradation was still evident. The U.S. Forest Service and other land-management agencies were limiting livestock numbers to match range conditions. However, the 1950s proved to be some of the driest years on record. Following a wet cycle in the late 1950s and early 1960s, our wild ungulate (hoofed) populations—mainly white-tailed and mule deer—reached an all-time high. This was due in part to the heavy persecution, by hunters, the livestock industry, and the state and federal governments, of the predators that preyed upon them. During the late 1950s and early 1960s, we saw areas where the deer browsed the leaves of the oaks up as high as they could reach, which gave portions of the forest a park-like appearance. The Arizona Game and Fish Department responded to these conditions by allowing the harvesting of does to help reduce deer numbers, but in spite of these efforts, a substantial die-off of both mule deer and white-tailed deer occurred.

During the 1960s, the sportsmen of Arizona encouraged the Arizona Game and Fish Department to classify mountain lions and black bears as big game animals, thus giving them some measure of protection. They also lobbied the government to curtail its predator-control activities by outlawing or limiting certain methods of take. The poison sodium fluoroacetate, commonly referred to as "1080," was banned, and restrictions were placed on "cyanide guns" (also known as "M-44 dispensers" or "cyanide traps"). Outdated versions of the M-44 called "coyote getters" that used a .38 caliber pistol cartridge for a triggering device were also banned.

The government also removed all bounties at this time. This eventually led to an increase in predator numbers, which helped to restore nature's ability to limit ungulate numbers. With these wildlife management changes and the changes in animal husbandry practices, we believe we see clear evidence that the lands are returning to their more "pristine" states.

But wait. What about the weather? Is man so egotistical as to think that he can control all conditions that affect our environment? The 1980s and 1990s saw rainfall totals at or above normal (especially in 1983 and 1993). As we were busily patting ourselves on the back as good land managers, the weather was restoring the plant and animal life. But what will the drought years of the 2000s bring? Without rainfall, all we can do as managers is try to lessen our impact on the land.

The pictures in this book are a testimony to the current healthy state of our Coronado National Forest lands now being managed under the multiple-use concept. They show diversity of species and healthy wildlife population numbers co-existing with sustainable livestock numbers, regulated mining, controlled hunting, and other recreational uses. Even though the project began after twenty years of good rainfall, these favorable conditions could not have existed without the constantly improving land-management methods in practice today.

Even now we are confronted daily by new and serious threats to our environment that we must continue to address. Uncontrolled land development, brought on by a rapidly exploding human population, is possibly our biggest problem. Illegal human activity tramples our grasslands, trashes our landscape, and disturbs wildlife. Global climate change and other unforeseen events loom. Believe it or not, our political system is designed to enable us to solve these problems. Scientists are publishing new information on environmental impacts every day. By utilizing this new information as it becomes available and laying aside personal agendas and partisan politics, we can overcome many of these threats. I continue to look at the condition of the land today as compared to what I saw in the 1950s, and my eyes truly see a pristine landscape.

When we hike and ride mountain trails, just knowing that we may see a jaguar track or possibly even a live jaguar certainly adds a bit of mystique to our adventure. The fact that resident jaguars are living in southeastern Arizona is testimony to the health and diversity of this unique landscape.

ANNA: The Curve in the Trail

As I sit here in our comfortable living room, I look up at a large picture of Macho B, made from a slide and placed on canvas to give the appearance of an oil painting. It was a housewarming gift from Emil and our rancher/photographer friend Scott Bell. Macho B's rosettes stand out against the background of a large, green lichen-covered boulder. The rosette we call "Pinocchio" is clearly visible on his right side. He pads stealthily along a forest path strewn with leaf litter, his eyes focused on what lies ahead. Below this picture is a smaller framed print of the same animal, a copy of a photo taken in August 1996, staring down at us from the safety of his branch in the alligator juniper tree.

Displayed on the couch across from the pictures is a beautiful needlepoint pillow, featuring an exact replica of the rosette on Macho B's left side that we've named "Betty Boop." Using a photo, our friend Loma created a pattern and then carefully stitched the rosette and others around it in perfect detail—a precious gift of love.

These all serve as reminders of the moment in August 1996 when we first encountered Macho B, and how our lives have dramatically changed since then. The jaguar dominates and influences our lives and will probably continue to do so. At this point, I would like to imitate Macho B in our large "oil painting," with eyes focused steadfastly on the path ahead and confidence in each step that we will take. Instead we find it is easy to allow our imaginations to run wild as we look to the future. Will we find a female jaguar? Will jaguar kittens dance in front of the camera lens? Do Machos C, D, and E now live in Arizona in remote areas with no camera surveillance? All these are questions that we and others can ask regarding what lies ahead in jaguar research.

As we look at the future realistically, we need to think of practical ways to collect more data on the jaguar in southeastern Arizona. We can envision expanding the number of cameras and the mountain ranges where they are placed, and we can be encouraged by the new awareness and emphasis on jaguar conservation in Mexico. We know that a radio-collared jaguar could tell us what corridors and habitat this animal is using as well as lead us directly to any female jaguars in this area.

Occasionally we travel east of the Rocky Mountains. As we visit our families in the Midwest, we soon tire of the predictable horizons and straight, flat roads of Iowa and North Dakota and become homesick for mountains and curving roads. There always seems to be a sense of adventure and the unknown when traveling a mountainous trail for the first time. The curve in the road can reveal the unexpected, a scene very similar to the one just traveled, or even a higher mountain to climb.

As true "Westerners," we really don't want to be able to see ahead on a straight, unbending road, tempting though it may be. In 1996, we rounded a curve in the trail and got ambushed, and nothing has been quite the same since then. So we will "hang on to our hats" and wait to see what is beyond the next bend. When we make the turn, we will no doubt be as astonished and surprised as we were in 1996.

/07   7:49 PM   BJDP

4/25/07   4:02 AM   B1a

Acknowledgments

We wish to thank the following individuals: David Lowell for planting the seed, Ross and Susan Humphreys of Rio Nuevo Publishers for pursuing the idea of a book and taking a chance on two amateur authors, Lisa Anderson and Caroline Cook for patience and skill in the editing process, and all those who worked on the design and completion of this book.

The Borderlands Jaguar Detection Project has been blessed with so many dedicated and excellent volunteers whom we cannot list individually in this limited space. Thank you each and every one.

A few dedicated souls have been with us from day one. Steve Bless located the funding that made it possible to begin the project and continues to monitor cameras. Janay Brun, alias Tigre Mujer, has become an excellent tracker, putting in countless hours in the field each month.

Muchas gracias to Emil McCain, project biologist. His bull-dog tenacity, tracking ability, and vast knowledge of the wild critters of the region elevate the status of the project far beyond our expectations.

As a boy, Matt Colvin followed Jack around the hills. Today his son, Levi Jack, now follows him. Matt and Levi monitored several of the cameras and transects. We could not have done it without them.

We are grateful for all the government agencies that partner and cooperate with us in our research, and who have enabled us to continue our research through funding.

Thanks to all the landowners and ranching groups who continue to be good stewards of the lands where we monitor big cats.

Above all we thank God for the "gift of the jaguar."

Detailed Species Descriptions

badger *(Taxidea taxus)*

range Western two-thirds of the U.S. and into Canada and Mexico (considered endangered in Canada; numbers declining in many parts of their range).

habitat Open flat areas easy to dig in; farmlands, grasslands, sandy plains near rivers.

physical characteristics Wide-bodied and short-legged; about 22 pounds; shaggy yellowish-brown coat with a white stripe on the forehead and down the nose; have "plantigrade" hind feet, meaning they walk flat-footed instead of just on their toes.

diet Strictly carnivorous: rabbits, gophers, ground squirrels, lizards, snakes, birds, eggs, carrion.

behavior Solitary, far-ranging; ferocious; nocturnal carnivores that dig to excavate their burrowing prey; find different dens to stay in every day.

life span 8–10 years.

reproduction Mate in July–August; 2–5 kits born in February–March; raised by the mother for 3 months.

bear, black or American black *(Ursus americanus)*

range Found throughout North America.

habitat Prefer forested and shrubby areas; may build dens in tree cavities, under rocks, in caves, or in shallow depressions.

physical characteristics About 5 feet long; weigh 90–400 pounds (females) or 110–700 pounds (males); coat color not always black, but may range from white to brown, especially west of the Mississippi River; keen sense of smell; usually walk on all fours, although they can stand on their hind legs.

diet Fruits, grasses, herbs, and insects such as ants, bees, and termites; opportunistic feeders, they will also eat carrion, fish, and honey, and catch small game including rodents, deer, javelinas, and livestock.

behavior Hibernate in winter; climb trees to avoid danger.

life span Up to 30 years.

reproduction Can breed by age 4–5, generally breed every 2–3 years in late spring, and 1–4 (but usually 2) cubs are not born until January or February; cubs stay with their mother for about a year.

bobcat *(Lynx rufus* or, more commonly, *Felis rufus)*

range All across the continental U.S.

habitat Wooded or brushy areas with thick vegetation and along washes, often near rocky areas; a single bobcat's home range may be just a few square miles; dens in small caves, under ledges, or in thick vegetation.

physical characteristics Adult bodies reach 2–3 feet in length; weigh 14–22 pounds.

diet Rabbits, mice, snakes, lizards, birds, and even small deer.

behavior Solitary (except for mating and mothers with kittens) and crepuscular; excellent climbers; can also swim; hunt by stalking or lying in ambush; usually have to hunt every day.

life span Up to 7 years.

reproduction Mate in spring; litters of 2–3 are born in late spring and raised by mother until fall.

buzzard *(see* vulture*)*

cattle *(Bos taurus)*

range Native to Europe and India; first introduced in southern Arizona and northern Sonora by Father Eusebio Francisco Kino in the late 1600s; many breeds present in the area now.

habitat All grasslands from desert scrub to alpine meadows.

physical characteristics Large bovid in the ox family, including cattle, sheep, goats, and antelope, having unbranched hollow horns and split hooves.

diet Grazers, feeding on both annual and perennial grasses and forbs; will eat saltbush and other woody plants if there's not enough grass.

behavior Live in herds consisting of cows and calves with a few bulls; primarily diurnal with feeding times at dawn and dusk, bedding at midday and at night.

life span Can live up to 15 years; on open range, cows are removed at end of their reproductive years (around age 10).

reproduction Can be born any time of the year, but calving peaks in spring and early summer; gestation about 9 months; one bull will mate with several cows and take no part in rearing young.

coati, white-nosed *(Nasua narica)*

range Arizona through Mexico and Central America and into western Colombia and Ecuador.

habitat Madrean oak woodlands, oak-sycamore canyons and riparian areas, occasionally into thick desert scrub; may move to lower elevations in winter.

physical characteristics Head and body 24 inches long, tail 19 inches long; weigh 10–15 pounds; long claws, very long tails are held vertically when they forage and run.

diet Omnivorous: eat grubs, beetles, and other invertebrates, along with nuts, fruit, rodents, eggs, snakes, lizards, and carrion. (White-nosed coatis in Arizona are primarily frugivorous, eating mostly juniper berries, grapes, and other riparian berries, plus beetles and grubs, caterpillars, centipedes, and scorpions.)

behavior Diurnal, most active in morning and late afternoon; females and their young live in social bands of 20 to 30 or more; make grunting and explosive "woof" sounds; forage both on the ground and in trees; sleep at night in trees or caves.

life span 7–14 years, or longer in captivity.

reproduction Adult males join the larger bands only for mating season (February–April); females bear 4–6 kits, usually nesting in a rock den or tree, raising them away from the rest of the band for the first six weeks.

cottontail, desert *(Sylvilagus audubonii)*

range Stay within a 400-square-yard home range.

habitat Thick, brushy areas with plenty of hiding places.

physical characteristics 1–2 pounds; have larger ears than most other cottontails.

diet Greenery such as grasses, forbs, mesquite leaves and beans, cactus, ornamental plants.

behavior Generally nocturnal, but will venture out in daytime in milder weather.

life span 2 years, though most are killed by predators in first year of life.

reproduction Breed throughout spring and summer; females can breed by 3 months of age and have multiple litters per year, helping to offset population losses due to heavy predation by other animals; babies are born blind, furless, and helpless, 2–4 per litter.

coyote *(Canis latrans)*

range Throughout North America below the Arctic.

habitat Just about anywhere, from cactus forests to urban areas, even golf courses.

physical characteristics Grow to 23–26 inches high at the shoulder; weigh 35–50 pounds in northern and eastern climates, and 15–30 pounds in western and southwestern climates; fur ranges from grayish to light brown.

diet Rodents, insects, birds, fish, carrion, cactus fruit, grass, berries, rabbits, snakes, deer, and occasionally livestock.

behavior Social animals that live, travel, and hunt in small family groups or packs of up to a dozen members; "sing" to communicate with neighbors, to keep track of family members, after rain, and during full moons; mark their territory by urinating and leaving scat, and also by marking the ground with scent glands on their paws; can run up to 30 miles an hour for short distances.

life span Up to 14 years.

reproduction Breed in February–March, 4–6 young born April–May; yearling pups may help their parents raise the next year's litter; average of 5 pups per litter.

deer, white-tailed (Coue's deer) *(Odocoileus virginianus couesi)*

range *Odocoileus virginianus* ranges throughout the U.S. and southern Canada; the smaller subspecies, Coue's deer, ranges in southeast Arizona, southwest New Mexico, and northern Mexico.

habitat From mesquite grasslands at approximately 3,200 feet upward through Madrean evergreen woodlands to evergreen forests at over 9,000 feet.

physical characteristics Bucks weigh 85–110 pounds, occasionally up to 125 pounds; does are approximately 25 percent smaller; bucks lose their antlers in April but regrow them by September.

diet Tree leaves including oak, juniper, mesquite; forbs and shrubs such as filaree, fairy duster, manzanita, mountain mahogany; and grasses; also fond of fruit from the barrel cactus, staghorn cholla, and prickly pear, and leaves of ocotillo.

behavior Herds consist of does and fawns; bucks live alone or in small groups; can run short distances at 35 miles per hour; active in morning, evening, and moonlit nights.

life span Up to 10 years.

reproduction Breed in winter; 1–2 fawns are born in summer, maturing in 12–18 months.

fox, gray *(Urocyon cinereoargenteus)*

range Eastern, Midwestern, and far western U.S.

habitat Prefers rocky canyons and brushy areas; like to den in caves, rock crevices, boulder piles, hollow logs, mine shafts, or other cavities—sometimes even badger burrows.

physical characteristics 14–15 inches high at shoulder; weigh 5–12 pounds; grayish coat with black stripe along top of tail.

diet Rodents, insects, birds, carrion, rabbits, snakes, berries, grasses, and fruits.

behavior These are the only canids able to climb trees, where they often sleep and hunt and forage; often leave scat to mark territory; nocturnal, quiet.

life span Up to 13 years.

reproduction Breed in late winter; pups born in March–April; mother stays in the den with pups while father guards it from a strategic vantage point; both parents feed the pups and teach them to hunt by 4 months of age.

horse *(Equus caballus)*

range Worldwide.

habitat Evolved in open grasslands; domesticated in Asia 6,000 years ago; horses now live in wide variety of climates and habitats, including urban areas.

physical characteristics 4–7 feet tall; 500–3,000 pounds; hoofed, speedy, and strong, with excellent sight and hearing; long mane and tail and short, coarse coat in colors ranging from white through shades of brown to black; sometimes spotted.

diet Herbivores; graze on grasses and eat other plant materials, including grain.

behavior Prey animal; live in herds organized in hierarchies; used by humans for work, transportation, sport, and occasionally food; may become feral.

life span 25–30 years.

reproduction Typically a single foal born in spring; may reproduce by age 3 but generally reach maturity between 4 and 6 years old; many distinct breeds.

human *(Homo sapiens sapiens)*

range Worldwide, with brief trips to the moon and outer space.

habitat Historically, near water and sources of food obtained either from hunting and gathering or from agriculture; more recently, humans have altered habitats for their own use, and human technology has enabled colonization of all continents and climates on Earth.

physical characteristics Bipedal primates 5–6 feet tall; 100–200 pounds; covered with short, nearly invisible hair except on scalp, face (males only), underarms, and pubic area, which are more heavily furred; skin color ranges from pale pink to dark brown; hair color from blond to black (often gray or white later in life); large, highly developed brain; upright posture frees hands for tools; usually wears clothing, which may indicate age, sex, occupation, status, and personality.

diet Omnivorous, occasionally herbivorous.

behavior Social and communicative; using mental processes, language, and tools, creates complex structures—physical, intellectual, and cultural.

life span 70–90 years in developed countries; 30 under hard conditions.

reproduction Breed year-round; infant born helpless, usually one at a time; requires years of care and reaches sexual maturity at age 12–15; approximate world population in 2007: 6.5 billion.

jaguar *(Panthera onca)*

range Present range extends from Mexico (with occasional sightings in southern Arizona and New Mexico) across much of Central America and south to Paraguay and northern Argentina; last documented in Texas in 1948.

habitat Dense jungle, chaparral scrublands, and timbered areas; southeastern Arizona sightings have occurred in oak woodland/mountainous terrain (elevations below 12,000 feet); make their dens in caves or dense thickets.

physical characteristics Largest cat of the New World; can reach 4 feet in length, plus a 20–30-inch tail; weigh 100–250 pounds; coat is usually orange buff, with black spots on the head and shoulders, and rosettes with one to three black dots inside the rosette on the back and flanks; white underbelly with black spots; black or "melanistic" individuals may appear in South and Central America.

diet Peccaries, deer, coatis, skunks, and other small mammals and carrion in the Southwest; in the tropics they feed on large ground-dwelling birds; sea-turtle eggs, fish, frogs, turtles, small alligators, capybara, tapir, and livestock.

behavior Nocturnal in the Southwest; solitary individuals are thought to wander as far as 500 miles; shy and will avoid confrontation with humans; fast runners for short distances, can also swim.

life span Up to 22 years.

reproduction Climate zones vary so much that there is no single mating season for all jaguars; in non-tropical areas, mating is more likely to occur when prey is plentiful; bear 2–4 young; the mother raises the young alone.

javelina or collared peccary *(Pecari tajacu or Tayassu tajacu)*

range Southwestern U.S. to South America.

habitat Prefer saguaro–palo verde forests or shrubby grasslands where there are prickly pear cacti, but also found in Madrean woodlands; generally have a territory of about 700–800 acres.

physical characteristics 20–24 inches tall; weigh 40–55 pounds; hooved; resembles a small boar, with long, sharp canine teeth; bristly coat is darker in winter, lighter in summer.

diet Prefer prickly pear cactus pads and fruits; also eat roots, tubers, seeds, mesquite pods, leaves, berries, and nuts; occasionally eat snakes, frogs, rodents, or carrion.

behavior Usually live and travel in groups of 5–15 (or more); chew their food as they amble along; with extremely poor vision, they rely on sense of smell to find and keep track of herd-mates, often marking each other with scent glands that yield a distinctive common scent for each herd; take dust and mud baths; nocturnal in summer, active during daytime in milder and cooler times of year; can gallop up to 25 miles an hour.

life span Up to 24 years.

reproduction Mothers usually bear two babies at a time, usually in summer, to coincide with summer rains and greening up of plants; babies can walk with the herd the day after birth.

lion, mountain *(Puma concolor* or *Felis concolor)*

range From Alaska to Tierra del Fuego.

habitat Forests of both desert and mountains; thick, rugged, brushy canyons or other secluded spots with good cover.

physical characteristics 75–145 pounds; can be 6 feet long, with a 3-foot, black-tipped tail; powerful hindquarters (have been known to leap 23 feet in one bound).

diet Deer, javelinas, bighorn sheep, coatis, rabbits, coyotes, squirrels, birds, other small mammals, livestock.

behavior Generally shy and elusive; cover larger kills with leaves and debris, returning daily to feed until prey is all consumed; rest during the day in small caves, thickets, or rocky areas; good climbers and swimmers.

life span Up to 15 years.

reproduction Breed at any time of year, starting at 2–3 years of age; 3–4 kittens are born after 3-month gestation and raised by the mother for up to 2 years.

opossum, Mexican brown-nosed *(Didelphis virginiana californica)*

range Has been slowly expanding its range northward; *Didelphis virginiana* (Virginia opossum) ranges across the U.S. and into Canada, but the Mexican subspecies seems to come from the south and is found in the southern border states.

habitat Can be found in a variety of habitats within its range, from relatively arid to riparian and swampland.

physical characteristics About the size of a large house cat; white to charcoal-colored fur, with brown stripes on face; "plantigrade" hind feet, meaning they walk flat-footed; hind feet have a clawless opposable digit; have prehensile tails that can grasp and assist with climbing.

diet Carrion, garbage, insects, worms, frogs, birds, and other small animals; also fruits and grains.

behavior Excellent climbers; nocturnal; nomadic, staying in an area as long as it provides enough food and water; when they "play possum," appearing to be dead when frightened, they are actually unconscious, as this is an involuntary physiological response; walk with a "pacing gait" (both left legs move at the same time, then both right legs move at the same time).

life span Thought to be 1–2 years.

reproduction Marsupial, meaning young are born at a very early stage and continue development in the mother's pouch for 2 more months; a bit later the mother may carry her babies on her back; up to 18 may be born at one time.

raccoon *(Procyon lotor)*

range Found across North America.

habitat Riparian or brushy and wooded areas near water; prefer thick vegetation.

physical characteristics 2–3 feet long, weigh 10–20 pounds; black face mask and a bushy, ringed tail.

diet Crayfish, small mammals, carrion, fruit and nuts, insects, eggs, fish, and garbage.

behavior Nocturnal and generally solitary; sometimes sleep in tree branches; known for being clever, sly, and mischievous; excellent climbers and can also swim; may use their extremely sensitive forepaws to examine their food before eating it.

life span 5–16 years.

reproduction Mating takes place January–March; 4–6 young are born 2 months later; males and females associate with each other only during mating; males may form small groups.

ringtail *(Bassariscus astutus)*

range Southwestern U.S.

habitat Rocky riparian canyons; less likely to be found in heavily wooded areas.

physical characteristics 24–30 inches long; 1–2.5 pounds; very large black eyes and big pink ears, long feathery tail with black and white rings; can rotate their hind paws 180 degrees to facilitate going face-first down steep cliff walls; use their strong tails for balance.

diet Mice and other rodents, insects, birds, lizards, snakes, and fruit.

behavior Nocturnal and solitary; excellent climbers and leapers; hide in crevices and hollow trees during the day.

life span up to 14 years.

reproduction Breeding occurs in April; 2–4 kits born in June; the young, raised by both parents, can hunt independently by fall.

skunk, hog-nosed *(Conepatus mesoleucus)*
skunk, hooded *(Mephitis macroura)*
skunk, Western spotted (*Spilogale gracilis*)
skunk, striped *(Mephitis mephitis)*

range Hog-nosed: southwestern U.S. and southern Texas into Central America. Hooded: southwestern U.S. borderlands south to Costa Rica. Western spotted: from southwestern Canada, Idaho, and southwest Wyoming, south to Mexico and west Texas. Striped: throughout the U.S.

habitat All habitats except for extreme desert; some differences among species, with striped skunk usually found in more open areas and spotted skunks in more rocky areas.

physical characteristics Hog-nosed (the least common skunk): 2–6 pounds; all white on top of the head, back, and tail; all black underneath; bare patch of skin on its long nose. Hooded: 20–30 inches long, 2–4 pounds; has a ruff of fur around the neck and highly variable stripe patterns—can be almost all black, or have a combination of side and back striped, or black with a white hood. Western spotted: the smallest of all skunk species, weighs about 1 pound; black and white pattern of broken stripes with a circle or triangle of white between the eyes. Striped: 20–30 inches long, weighs 2–10 pounds; usually two stripes down back, occasionally all-white back or short stripes over shoulders; white-tipped black tail. All species have "plantigrade" hind feet, meaning they walk flat-footed instead of just on their toes, with a shuffling, waddling gait.

diet These opportunistic omnivores eat anything including worms, grubs, beetles, grasshoppers, mice and other rodents, birds and eggs, carrion, seeds, fruit; usually gain extra weight in fall to help survive winter (though they don't hibernate).

behavior All species are nocturnal; will either build their own dens or move in with other animals such as pack rats, or simply use hollow logs, brush piles, mine shafts, or crawl spaces under buildings. Most can spray their foul musk 10–15 feet, but they are slow to anger and will give warning before spraying. All may stay underground for several days at a time during cold winter storms. Western spotted is the only skunk that climbs trees.

life span 2–10 years.

reproduction Hog-nosed, hooded, and striped: breeding takes place in spring, 3–7 kits born in May and stay with mother through their first summer. Western spotted: breed in September or October, but young are not born until May; the 3–7 kits in a litter stay with the mother through summer.

squirrel, Arizona gray *(Sciurus arizonensis)*
squirrel, Rock *(Spermophilus variegatus)*

range Arizona gray: central to southeastern Arizona; also found in some New Mexico canyons and northern Sonora, Mexico. Rock squirrel: Arizona, New Mexico, west Texas, and parts of Nevada, Utah, and Colorado, down into Mexico.

habitat Arizona gray: primarily in elevations over 5,000 feet; deciduous forests with walnut, oak, and pine trees. Rock squirrel: rocky outcroppings, canyon walls, rock piles, tree roots, and urban areas; rocky terrain from high mountains to desert edges, throughout the southwest U.S. and northern Mexico.

physical characteristics Arizona gray: 16–22 inches long; weighs 1–2.5 pounds; gray fur with a light underbelly; coat is a little darker in winter; long bushy tail may serve as a blanket in extreme cold. Rock squirrel: weighs up to 1.5 pounds (one of the largest of the ground squirrels).

diet Arizona gray: walnuts, acorns, pine cone seeds, berries, seeds, and fungi; stores food to eat in winter (does not hibernate). Rock squirrel: seeds, mesquite pods and flowers, insects, birds and eggs, carrion, nuts, and fruit (including cactus fruit).

behavior Arizona gray: most active in morning and late afternoon; freezes in place to avoid being detected; makes a nest of leaves in a tree for raising the babies; several squirrels at once may harvest nuts in the same tree; they may also share nests. Rock squirrel: these ground-dwellers den in rocky crevices and talus slides, or dig burrows between buried boulders to retreat to for safety but spend most of their days on the surface, foraging and getting sun; retreat to the burrow during cold winter periods, but are not believed to truly hibernate; excellent climbers; most active at dawn and dusk; live in colonies of numerous females and their young, defended by a nearby dominant male.

life span Arizona gray squirrels may live 12 years, but most don't live longer than 6 years if they survive the dangerous first year of life. Rock squirrel: 4–5 years.

reproduction Arizona gray: breeds April–May; 2–4 babies born two months later. Rock squirrel: mate in early spring; babies born in March and sometimes again in August or September, depending on how severe or mild the local winters are.

turkey, Gould's *(Meleagris gallopavo mexicana)*

range Various mountain ranges of southern Arizona and New Mexico; also in the Sierra Madre mountains of Mexico; had been eradicated in Arizona but are back due to a reintroduction effort by Arizona Game and Fish and other organizations.

habitat Mountains; use open areas for feeding and mating, and forested areas for roosting and hiding.

physical characteristics 8–12 pounds (hens) or 16–22 pounds (toms); have longer legs, larger feet, and larger center tail feathers than any other wild turkey in North America; males have large spurs on the backs of their feet for defense.

diet 90 percent of food is from plants such as grasses, forbs, vines, seeds, fruits, and acorns; will also consume crops such as corn, wheat, soybeans, oats, and clover; also eat insects and small invertebrates such as snakes and frogs.

behavior Can run as fast as 26 miles an hour and fly up to 55 miles an hour; spend most of their time on the ground but roost in trees; tend to venture out in flocks, foraging in early morning and late afternoon.

life span 5–6 years.

reproduction Breed between February and April; 10–13 eggs are laid about 2 weeks later.

vulture, black *(Coragyps atratus)*

vulture, turkey, or turkey buzzard *(Cathartes aura)*

range Black vulture: southeastern U.S. and southern Arizona, south to Brazil. Turkey vulture: throughout U.S. and into southern Canada, migrating as far as South America.

habitat Garbage dumps, beaches, open country, woodlands, around human settlements.

physical characteristics Black vulture: 22–26 inches long, wingspan 59 inches, weighs about 4.4 pounds; shiny, black bird with gray head and feet; shorter, more square tail than the turkey vulture's; large silvery patch on each wing tip; regurgitates when threatened. Turkey vulture: 26-–30 inches long; wingspan 67 inches, weighs 4 pounds; undersides of wings are two-toned black and white; reddish head and feet, rest of body is dark brown to black. Both species cool themselves by urinating on their own legs.

diet Primarily carrion.

behavior Black vulture: very social, usually seen in pairs or small groups, may mix with turkey vultures or follow them to carrion; wings nearly flat when soaring; when flying, wingbeats are snappy and quick in a flap-flap-flap-short glide pattern; often spread wings while roosting, nest in caves, tree stumps, on a cliff face, or other hidden areas. Turkey vulture: may hunt singly or in groups; goes for long periods gliding or soaring on thermals without moving its wings; may tilt or rock from side to side while soaring; its wingbeats are deep and smooth; flies low while hunting, using keen sense of smell to locate prey; makes a hissing sound when threatened.

life span As long as 20–25 years.

reproduction Black vulture: 1–3 pale greenish eggs; eggs may be found in nests January–July and are incubated by both parents for 37–41 days. Turkey vulture: lays 1–3 whitish eggs with brown and gray markings, March–June; eggs are incubated by both parents for 34–41 days. Both species: a male–female pair may stay together and raise successive clutches of babies for many years.

Additional Reading and Selected Websites

Brown, David E., and Carlos A López González. *Borderland Jaguars: Tigres de la Frontera.* Salt Lake City, Utah: University of Utah Press, 2001.

Childs, Jack. *Tracking the Felids of the Borderlands.* El Paso, Texas: Printing Corner Press, 1998.

Davis, Goode P. Jr. *Man and Wildlife in Arizona: The American Exploration Period, 1824–1865.* Ed. Neil B. Carmony and David E. Brown. Phoenix, Arizona: Arizona Game & Fish Department, 2001.

Glenn, Warner. *Eyes of Fire: Encounter with a Borderlands Jaguar.* El Paso, Texas: Printing Corner Press, 1996.

Hansen, Kevin. *Cougar: The American Lion.* Flagstaff, Arizona: Northland Publishing, 1992.

———. *Bobcat: Master of Survival.* New York: Oxford University Press, 2007.

Logan, Kenneth A., and Linda L. Sweaner. *Desert Puma: Evolutionary Ecology and Conservation of an Enduring Carnivore.* Washington, D.C.: Island Press, 2001.

Quinn, Meg. *Wildflowers of the Desert Southwest.* Tucson, Arizona: Rio Nuevo Publishers, 2000.

Rabinowitz, Alan. *Jaguar: One Man's Struggle to Establish the World's First Jaguar Preserve.* New York: Arbor House, 1986.

Sayre, Nathan F. *Working Wilderness: The Malpai Borderlands Group and the Future of the Western Range.* Tucson, Arizona: Rio Nuevo Publishers, 2005.

Shaw, Harley. *Soul Among Lions: The Cougar as Peaceful Adversary.* Boulder, Colorado: Johnson Publishing Company, 1989.

———. *Mountain Lion Field Guide,* Special Report #9, Arizona Game & Fish Department, fourth printing, 1990.

Spellenberg, Richard. *Sonoran Desert Wildflowers.* Helena, Montana: Falcon/Globe Pequot Press, 2003.

Swinburne, Stephen R. *The Woods Scientist.* Boston, Massachusetts: Houghton Mifflin Co., 2002.

Taylor, Ronald J. *Desert Flowers of North America.* Missoula, Montana: Mountain Press Publishing Co., 1998.

www.azgfd.gov/w_c/es/jaguar_management.shtml

www.gf.state.az.us/ (for history of individual mammal species click on Hunting & Fishing/Big Game Species or Small Game Species and select mammal)

www.borderjag.org/

www.bear-tracker.com/mammals.html

www.easterncougarnet.org/newsletter.html

www.cdc.gov/ncidod/dvrd/rabies/

http://wcslivinglandscapes.com/about

http://savethejaguar.com/jag-index

Rio Nuevo Publishers®
P.O. Box 5250, Tucson, Arizona 85703-0250
(520) 623-9558, www.rionuevo.com

Library of Congress Cataloging-in-Publication Data

Childs, Jack L.
  Ambushed on the jaguar trail : hidden cameras on the Mexican border / Jack L. and Anna Mary Childs.
     p. cm.
  Includes bibliographical references.
  ISBN 978-1-933855-09-7
  1. Jaguar—Arizona. 2. Jaguar—Mexican-American Border Region. 3. Childs, Jack L. 4. Childs, Anna Mary. 5. Chronophotography. 6. Wildlife photography. I. Childs, Anna Mary. II. Title.
  QL737.C23C457 2007
  599.75'5—dc22
                                    2007038937

Design: Karen Schober, Seattle, Washington.

Printed in Korea.

10 9 8 7 6 5 4 3 2 1